Awakening
Mystical Consciousness

Other Writings of Joel S. Goldsmith

Awakening
Mystical Consciousness

Joel S. Goldsmith

Edited By
Lorraine Sinkler

I-Level
An Imprint of Acropolis Books, Publisher

Lakewood, CO   Austell, GA

Acropolis Books, Inc.
747 Sheridan Blvd., Suite 1A, Lakewood, Colorado 80214-2551
(303) 231-9923 ~ In USA (800) 771-9923
http://www.acropolisbooks.com

Library Of Congress Cataloging-In-Publication Data

Goldsmith, Joel S. , 1892–1964.
    Awakening mystical consciousness / Joel S. Goldsmith ; edited by
Lorraine Sinkler.
            p.   cm.
    Originally published: San Francisco : Harper & Row, 1980.
    Includes bibliographical references and index.
    ISBN 1-889051-06-3 (alk. paper)
    1. New Thought.   2. Mysticism   I. Sinkler, Lorraine.   II. Title.

BF639.G5573   1997
299' .93 – – dc21   96-40301
                                                                  CIP

This book is printed on acid free paper that meets standard Z 39.48 of
the American National Standards Institute

Except the Lord build the house,
they labour in vain that build it.
—Psalm 127

"Illumination dissolves all material ties and binds men together with the golden chains of spiritual understanding; it acknowledges only the leadership of the Christ; it has no ritual or rule but the divine, impersonal universal Love; no other worship than the inner Flame that is ever lit at the shrine of Spirit. This union is the free state of spiritual brotherhood. The only restraint is the discipline of Soul; therefore, we know liberty without license; we are a united universe without physical limits, a divine service to God without ceremony or creed. The illumined walk without fear—by Grace."

—The Infinite Way by Joel S. Goldsmith

TABLE OF CONTENTS

THE ATHEISM OF MATERIAL POWER
BEING A DISCIPLE OF THE CHRIST — LIVING OUT FROM THE PRINCIPLE OF ONE SELF — LIVING BY THE WORD — PRAYING TO A SPIRITUAL GOD TO CHANGE A MATERIAL UNIVERSE — THE SILENCE

RELEASING SPIRITUAL POWER
THE UNKNOWN QUANTITY — DISCOVERING THE NATURE OF SPIRITUAL POWER — RISING ABOVE THE LEVEL OF THE PROBLEM — THE NATURE OF SPIRITUAL SELFHOOD — EVIDENCING SPIRITUAL POWER — REALIZING THE PRESENCE OF GOD AS OMNIPRESENCE — THE ULTIMATE GOAL OF THE REVELATION OF SPIRITUAL POWER — PURIFYING OUR STATE OF CONSCIOUSNESS

SPIRITUAL POWER UNVEILED
A FEAR-RIDDEN WORLD — THE NATURE OF SPIRITUAL POWER — THE FOLLY OF FIGHTING TEMPORAL POWER — PROVING SPIRITUAL POWER IS THE ALL-POWER — THE OPEN SESAME — OVERCOMING THE WORLD — FUNCTION OF THE CHRIST

PART II. THE WORD MADE FLESH

FLESH AND FLESH
THE INVISIBLE WORD BECOMES TANGIBLE — THE FLESH THAT WITHERS — REVEALING THE WORD — DO NOT GLORY IN THE FORM — KNOWING PERSONS SPIRITUALLY — BEING CLOTHED WITH A NEW CONCEPT OF BODY — A STATE OF AWARENESS

TABLE OF CONTENTS

TABLE OF CONTENTS

PREFACE

FREQUENTLY a reader who has discovered Joel Goldsmith's books makes the comment, "This is not like reading a book. It is as if the author were right here talking directly to me." Such a reaction is quite natural because of the way Joel Goldsmith's books were written. Never, except for parts of *The Infinite Way*,* did Joel actually sit down to write a book. He was far too busy for that. His time was spent in answering the calls for healing that came day and night from all over the world and in teaching those who wanted to learn more about healing and about attaining the mystical consciousness.

In 1946, Joel Goldsmith went through an initiation into the hidden mysteries of life, a deep spiritual experience that lifted him out of the metaphysical realm into the mystical union of conscious oneness with the Source of life. With that experience came the demand to teach those who came to him, though never to seek a student.**

From then on, he was strengthened by the Spirit within him, which instructed him and brought the work of each day—work that included answering enormous amounts of mail from those who had found his message

---

*by the Author
**Lorraine Sinkler, *The Spiritual Journey of Joel S. Goldsmith* (New York, Harper & Row, 1973), p. 143.

xi

and sought him out. In the brief span of seventeen years, he gave hundreds of classes throughout the world. With the advent of the tape recorder, these lectures and classes were recorded for posterity. Furthermore, a great many of them have been edited and published in book form.

When Joel gave a lecture or a class, he spoke extemporaneously, without even a single note. This did not mean that he had made no preparation; his preparation consisted of long hours of meditation before each class. He meditated not for a subject or a specific lesson, but that he might be completely immersed in the Spirit and thereby be a transparency for It to pour forth as the appropriate message. His message, therefore, is always fresh and new; it came directly out of consciousness and was delivered in a natural, simple, direct, and forceful manner, and with the authority of one who proved by his works the truth of the message he taught.

Awakening Mystical Consciousness was originally published in the form of Letters sent out each month to students of The Infinite Way. The material used for these Letters was taken from his recorded classes. At the end of this book, the classes used in the preparation of *Awakening Mystical Consciousness* are listed for those who wish to go deeper into the message. A further aid to study is the index, prepared by Barbara Griffiths.

Joel Goldsmith was admirably qualified to speak and write of the mystical consciousness. With him it was not intellectual knowledge gleaned from reading speculative philosophy on the meaning of life; it was an experience. He was able to clothe his message with a simplicity that could come only through a realized consciousness of oneness which permitted no duality.

For him, the mystical life meant living in the world, but not being of it, partaking of many of the activities of normal living, yet always reserving an area of consciousness to penetrate beyond the outer world of effect to the underlying spiritual reality. He saw beyond the visible to the invisible Source of all life and activity.

One of the fundamental principles of The Infinite Way is that the mystical experience, which is what The Infinite Way really is, can never be limited by or bound within the confines of an organization. For that reason, there is nothing to which anyone can belong; there are no rules or regulations except "the discipline of Soul," governing anyone who embraces its principles. Each one is free to come and go or to remain a part of this movement in consciousness, dedicated to awakening the mystical consciousness within every person and eventually revealing the hereness and nowness of the Kingdom of Heaven.

LORRAINE SINKLER
Palm Beach, Florida

PART I.

THE NATURE OF
SPIRITUAL POWER

~ 1 ~

THE ATHEISM OF MATERIAL POWER

FEAR grips humanity because fear, implanted in the mind of man, has made man forget God is the life of man and that life cannot be destroyed, not by a bomb or by the will of tyrants. Mesmeric world suggestion makes man think he has a life of his own and it can be lost. Humanly, this is true. Spiritually, under the Christ, it is not. The Master let his human life be taken, and then he proved that neither his life nor his body could be destroyed. Neither our individual life nor our body can be destroyed by human will or deed when we know the truth about life.

In the London blitz during World War II, one couple agreed that because they had accepted God as their life, their safety, and their security, they would not build a bombproof shelter as had all their neighbors. Each evening when the blitz began and their neighbors went to their shelters, they volunteered for fire watch and walked up and down the streets. Not only were they not touched, but neither was their home, even though all around it there was great destruction. It did not come near their dwelling place for the simple reason that their dwelling place was not London, a house, or a bomb-proof shelter. Their dwelling place was God; they lived and moved and had their being in God.

"The Lord is my rock, and my fortress."[1] Many persons believe that means God will send them a brick or cement fortress. It does not mean that at all. It means what it says, that it is God in whom "we live, and move, and have our being."[2] But the human race has cut itself off from that fortress of God by seeking safety and security in pieces of matter.

BEING A DISCIPLE OF THE CHRIST

The disciples of the Christ were imprisoned, but they walked out of prison with an angel ministering to them.[3] The disciple of the Christ, who does not believe safety, security, health, and harmony are to be found in pieces of matter, mounts the cross and rises out of the tomb. That individual, reborn of the Spirit, lives in the Fourth Dimension of life. He is still in the world but not of it. The disciple of the Christ moves about in the world and works at the same daily tasks as others do, whether it be in business, in a household, or in the arts or professions; but he is not subject to its beliefs, its fears, or its powers. The Master said, "I pray not that thou shouldest take them out of the world, but that thou shouldest keep them from the evil."[4]

"In the world ye shall have tribulation."[5] This tribulation exists because the world believes in all kinds of powers: the power of heredity, the power of sin, the power of disease, the power of bombs, the power of wars, the power of false appetites, and the power of weather and climate. But when the Master said his disciples were to be left in the world but would not be subject to its powers, he gave the pattern for us to follow.

Our prayer is that we be left in the world that we may be a light unto persons who still fear to die, as if the experience of death were going to be the end of life. No matter how close to God a person may be, each one sooner or later leaves this plane; but unless he fears extinction, there is nothing to fear in that transitional experience. As the light of the world, those who have attained the mystical consciousness are revealing to this world that there is no need to fear the powers of this world.

I can tell you how to gauge your spiritual progress. As long as you believe destroying another life to save your own is justifiable, you are in that state of humanhood that is concerned only with its own self rather than with the one Self. As long as you are willing to destroy another life to save yours, you do not understand the message of Jesus Christ, which says, "Greater love hath no man than this, that a man lay down his life for his friends."[6]

LIVING OUT FROM THE PRINCIPLE OF ONE SELF

In World War I, I volunteered with the United States Marines; and although at that time I was a young student of metaphysics, I had learned it is possible to protect myself from the powers of this world by hiding myself in the Christ, where no evil power can come near me. I prayed that way for weeks, until one day I was struck by how horrible God must be if, by reciting abracadabra, I could be protected while all the persons who did not know about it would go out and get killed. There I would be with my gun, killing right and left, and I could not be touched. But the poor fellows who did not know about this wonderful prayer could die. I could not believe there was such a God, and I realized there was something wrong with that form of prayer. Not knowing any other, I decided not to pray again until I had learned how to pray correctly.

Days went by, and I refused to engage in any such protective prayer until one day, by an apparent accident, I knocked my Bible to the floor. It fell open to this passage: "Neither pray I for these alone."[7] The weight fell off my heart and shoulders, and I said, "Thank You, Father. Never again will I pray for me or for mine alone. But now my prayer is that the grace of God encompass mankind, that the grace of God touch every living soul to the spiritual life."

A miracle took place as far as I was concerned. I was transferred from one place to another, from one duty to another; and never once during the war was I sent anywhere near where I could shoot anybody or be shot at. I saw then that not only was there protection for me, there was also protection from me. Since then, I have learned a tremendous lesson, which I have set forth in the chapter "Love Thy Neighbor" in *Practicing the Presence.** The principle is that there is but one Self, and that is the God-Self.

The life of God is my life and yours; the soul of God is my soul and yours; the Spirit of God is my spirit and yours; the very selfhood of God is my selfhood and your selfhood, and that means we are one in spiritual sonship. Anything that benefits me must benefit you; anything that harms me must harm you, for we are one. Anything I do that is a blessing to me must be a blessing

---

*By the Author

to you; and anything that is a blessing to you must be a blessing to me, for we are one.

If I do anything destructive to you, I am doing it to myself, for there is but one. If I do anything of a withholding nature, I am not withholding from you; I am withholding from me. If I do anything destructive, I am not destroying you; I am destroying me, for we are one. We often wonder why we are paying the penalty of sickness, sin, or poverty, not realizing what we have done to humanity.

To the world, there is only one way of doing and that is by deeds. The world does its good and it does its evil by deeds, but that is not true of you or me. Even if we refrained from evil deeds, it would not be enough. Even if we did good deeds, it would not be enough. Paul said if we did all the good on earth but had not love, it would be nothing.[8] And the Master told us that if we committed none of these sins and yet allowed them to enter our thought, we were sinners: "Whosoever looketh on a woman to lust after her hath committed adultery with her already in his heart."[9]

So it is that good deeds are not enough for us. Refraining from evil deeds is not enough. We must go one step further and bear no false witness against our neighbor. Silently and secretly, we must realize that God is the life of every individual, whether or not he or she knows it and lives by it. The very moment we begin to know the truth that God is the life of everyone, that God's grace is sufficient unto all people everywhere, when we begin to pray for those who are wrecking this world–pray that the grace of God open their soul and consciousness to the truth of being, pray that the light of God touch their darkened consciousness, pray that everyone be an instrument through which God can freely operate–then and then only do you and I begin to "die daily"[10] to the human ways of life and experience a rebirth as children of God who no longer have to take thought for their life, but who now live by Grace.

LIVING BY THE WORD

Our life on the spiritual path is in part an inspirational experience, always followed by a practical living demonstration of God's harmony. Everything we read in Scripture that comes with the power and force of revelation becomes a principle to be used in our lifework of attaining conscious union with the Source.

Basic to that is the mystical statement, "The Word was made flesh, and dwelt among us."[11] We try insofar as it is possible to have our entire experience based not only on God, but lived in God, in the Word, so our daily activity becomes God in action. The word of God becomes tangible in our experience. We do not live a life separate and apart from God. On the contrary, any phase of our life that has its basis in our human will or human desire we find ultimately to be an unhappy and unprofitable experience.

Suppose we have awakened this morning knowing that ahead of us lies a strenuous day, a day in which many demands will be made upon us, demands probably of an extraordinary nature, some of which we will not be able to fill. It may be one of those days when we know we are not up to what the day is going to bring forth; so in accord with our living in the Word and letting the Word live in us, we turn within our consciousness for some unfoldment, some revelation, some

Word that is to come from the kingdom of God within our own being.

If we are patient and sincerely realize that there is a kingdom of God within us and that the Word can impart Itself to us from within, eventually it will come, at first not so easily, but with practice, readily. Then we may feel or hear within ourselves: "The Lord will perfect that which concerneth me."[12] Immediately, a sense of release comes to us; the responsibility falls away because now we have been given the assurance that the burden is not on our shoulders exclusively. With that, we will probably remember also that "greater is he that is in you, than he that is in the world."[13] He that is within me is greater than any problem that can face me this day; He that is within me is greater than any demand that can be made upon me. Now we have the very word of God abiding in our consciousness, and no longer do we face the day alone, but with God.

There is not a business problem of any kind that cannot be solved in this manner. Persons who try to run a business by themselves may be successful, may fail, or may be just a nominal success; but the business will always be subject to the conditions of the day. Persons who live in contact with this inner Fire, abiding in the Word and letting the Word abide in them, however, have no concern about business except to do what is given them to do each day. They find that, good times or bad times, provision is always made to carry them through successfully.

When an individual begins to surrender himself to God, seeking always to know the will of God and to be an instrument for Its fulfillment, the word of God becomes the very Christ in the midst of him which enables him to be a light unto this world and a servant unto everyone.

As we keep our consciousness filled with the word of God, we attract the harmony, peace, prosperity, health, and grace that flow from God. In proportion as we live our life separate from the word of God do we bring the world's experience of lack, limitation, war, discord, or inharmony to ourselves.

As we let the Word abide in us, the Word will become flesh and dwell among us; and peace and prosperity will be the law unto our household. If we neglect to establish ourselves in the Presence—getting up in the morning, bathing, dressing, going to work, running a household—and do not fill our consciousness with this word of God we are likely to become victims of everything that happens in the world. Then we go back to our old pagan ideas of blaming God. But God never forsakes us: we forsake God. There is no better way to forsake God than to believe God's influence is not greater than the influence of a bomb, a germ, or a tyrant.

The moment we begin to fear any power, whether the power of a person, a thing, or an ideology, we have forsaken God. When we allow fear of our body or fear of ill health to enter our thought, we have forsaken God, for we have forsaken the inner realization and knowledge we each must have that God is greater than these. We fear only because we believe that what we fear has more power than the God we worship.

PRAYING TO A SPIRITUAL GOD TO CHANGE
A MATERIAL UNIVERSE

God is Spirit; and if God is the creative principle of the universe, then this universe is a spiritual creation, not a physical or a corporeal one. If that is true, it is foolish to pray to a spiritual God to do something to a physical universe that does not have any real existence.

We are dreaming when we pray to a spiritual God to change some kind of matter or some physical structure. God is not in that picture. The prayer should be, "Awake thou that sleepest, and arise from the dead, and Christ shall give thee light."[14] Then whatever is necessary to awaken us from the dream of a physical or mechanical universe takes place, and we begin to come into our full heritage as the children of God, offspring of the Spirit, eternal and immortal.

We need more persons to whom we can turn for help who will sit down and not try to reduce a fever, remove a lump, stay paralysis, or stop insanity. Instead they will realize that God is Spirit, that the offspring of God is spiritual, and into that creation nothing enters that "defileth . . . or maketh a lie."[15]

Students of The Infinite Way do not deal with the body from a structural standpoint. This is a spiritual universe, and God alone is power. It is a form of atheism to fear any form of matter. It is an acknowledgment that all is not spiritual. Trying to change a material universe or trying humanly to interfere with what is going on in the world will get us nowhere. There is no permanent peace in fighting the evils of the world with the weapons of the world. The way is "not by might, nor by power, but by my spirit."[16] "Ye shall not need to fight in this battle: set yourselves, stand ye still, and see the salvation of the Lord."[17] Neither the mental weapons nor the physical weapons of this world are power. If they are or if there is not somebody to demonstrate that they are not, this world is lost.

But whose responsibility is this? Is it not that of those who know the truth and are awake to prove that the evils of the world are not power? But these evils cannot be stopped except by the realization of the nothingness or the nonpower of what is claimed to be great power. We cannot expect to do this unless we are willing to set aside enough time each day to sit down and look at some form of error—some form of sin or disease—look right at it and know:

You are not power: you are the carnal mind, or nothingness; you are the "arm of flesh," [18] or nothingness. You could have no power unless it came from God, for there is no power but God. God is the life of all being, the immortality and the eternality. God is the only law, the only lawgiver. There is no law of matter; there is no law of disease. Material power is not power: it is a claim of power. God, Spirit, is power; and Spirit is infinite, all power. *

Unless we are specific in our knowing of the truth, specific in our realization that we are being confronted with suggestions of mental and physical powers that are

---

*The italicized portions of this book are spontaneous meditations that came to the author during periods of uplifted consciousness. They are not in any sense intended to be used as affirmations, denials, or formulas. They have been inserted to serve as examples of the free flowing of the Spirit. As readers practice the Presence, they too, in their exalted moments, will receive ever new and fresh inspiration as the outpouring of the Spirit.

not powers, they will continue to be powers until we have the realization of their nonpower.

In most of our work, healings come quickly and joyously. The principle involved is the realization that to believe material power is power is nothing but atheism. God is Spirit, and spiritual power is the only real power. Any other claim of power can be reversed or nullified. We have witnessed this in the healing of every type of problem. Where necessary, forms of matter, forms of physical body, have changed; and, where necessary, new parts of the body have grown because Spirit is the underlying substance and reality of all effect.

In the presence of spiritual realization, materiality is not power. Whether it appears as infection or contagion, whether it appears as hypnotism or the product of hypnotism, it is the mind of flesh or the "arm of flesh." It is therefore nothingness, for Spirit is the all and the real and the eternal. Spirit is the law.

For the sake of Infinite Way work all around the world and most of all for the sake of the world itself in its present state, it is important that every Infinite Way student sit down and begin to do some healing work to prove that sin, disease, and death are not the law or the reality of life. Proving mental and physical laws are not power will make possible the greater work of nullifying all forms of hypnotism that seem to emanate from individuals in high places and hold people in bondage. We must nullify every mental and physical claim of power wherever we meet up with it. We must accept it as a responsibility that wherever our attention is drawn to mental or physical power, we will sit down quietly and peacefully and realize that "not by might, nor by power," but by the Spirit of God is all of this made null and void.

Wherever we may be, that is holy ground, the place God has given to us for our worship. Our worship consists of the realization of the invisible Spirit as the law and the cause of all that is. Through this realization, without using mental might or physical power, every claim of an atheistic nature can be met and destroyed. It is destroyed, not by fighting, not by battling, not by asking God to do something, but by quietly, peacefully, and gently realizing, "Thank You, Father, this is Your universe, spiritual, complete, and whole."

Anything else that may be necessary for us to know will be given from within ourselves. Once we have attained or achieved the ability to be still and quiet, we will only have to start the flow with some of these truths that we know. But the real power, the real treatment, will come from within us to ourselves. What is imparted to us from within is the Word that is quick, sharp, and powerful.

THE SILENCE

Regardless of how we may feel when we go into meditation, eventually we settle down into an inner peace; and when we do, we are at the important part of our meditation because the power of God is made manifest in that period when the human mind is not thinking. Knowing the truth is not what heals, it is what takes place when we are through consciously knowing or thinking the truth. Then, in that period of stillness, the word of God comes through.

Declaring the truth is only a process of getting ready for an inner stillness and listening, and then either some thought comes to us or there is just a feeling that is sometimes more important than any words. When that feeling, which may be like a release or a deep breath, comes, the Spirit Itself * is taking over in our experience. The greatest healing works, the greatest works of restoration and reformation, and the greatest works of spiritual power are accomplished when there is neither word nor thought, when there is a complete stillness. Then something, the revelation of the Spirit and Its power, takes place within.

Spiritual illumination and spiritual power come through a complete silencing of human thought, human will, and human desire. In that complete absence of self, when there is only an inner peace, an expectance, there comes that little jump, that little deep breath, that little gasp, that little release. That is when we know the Spirit is on the field and the work is being accomplished.

It is egotism to believe our understanding ever accomplishes healing work. It is an upsurge from within, and a Presence and a Power that reveals Itself in stillness, in quietness, and in calmness, that does the work.

God reaches us in the silence. We have been told there is no power in the storm, the lightning, or the thunder but only in the "still small voice."[19] That is where the power of God is, in the "still small voice" uttered within us when we are still and listening, peaceful, quiet, and assured. The kingdom of God is within us, and It utters Itself. It may utter Itself in speech; It

---

*In the spiritual literature of the world, the varying concepts of God are indicated by the use of such words as *Father, Mother, Soul, Spirit, Principle, Love,* and *Life.* Therefore, in this book, the author has used the pronouns *He* and *It,* or *Himself* and *Itself,* interchangeably in referring to God.

may utter Itself as a light; It may utter Itself merely as an inner glow. But when It does, something happens.

When we enter meditation, we have only one obligation, and that is to forget anybody and everybody in this world, to turn within and realize the kingdom of God is within us. In the quietness and confidence of meditation, nobody or nobody's problem enters our mind. All the Father has will be released through the "still small voice."

In such a meditation, I am not thinking of any person; I am not thinking of anyone's problem; I am not thinking of myself. I am just being still and waiting for some sign from within that tells me God is on the field. And I wait until it comes—a catching of the breath, a feeling of peace, a sense of inner release. Then I know something has taken place because the word of God, the presence of God, the breath has gone out from me.

Jesus said, "I perceive that virtue is gone out of me,"[20] and the woman was healed. He felt that release of something out into the world, and the receptive and responsive experienced it. It is said that multitudes were healed as they sat listening to him. We may be sure he did not know their names or their particular sins, diseases, or problems. He was not thinking of them. His entire thought was on one subject: God. And as he sat in his silent communion with God, or even when he was giving a lesson, he was still maintaining that inner silence. Some had instantaneous healings, and some felt the Spirit so powerfully upon them that they had spiritual regeneration. Others may have come back two, three, or four times before they realized either a physical healing or spiritual regeneration.

Since the beginning of history, good and evil have been at war. For us, the battle between good and evil is stopped only as we understand the nature of spiritual power and retire into this quiet peaceful center of our own being and are at peace until the Spirit of God is upon us. In that silence, the Holy Ghost descends, and healing of all kinds can take place: reformation, healing of the body, or healing of war.

The Holy Ghost cannot descend upon us while we are a mind divided against itself. The Holy Ghost can descend only where the mind that was in Christ Jesus is present, the mind that never condemns or judges. Only when our mind has settled down into an inner peace in which there is no judgment, no condemnation, in which there is neither good nor evil because all emanates from God, can the Holy Ghost descend and the healing influence flow outward. We must not go into the inner Self double-minded, knowing good and evil.

Outwardly, we may realize we are dealing with the appearance of good and evil. Certainly, if we did not realize that, we would be blinded and we would be somewhat in the attitude of those who just walk around saying, "There is no evil. All is God," and then all of a sudden find themselves thrown overboard.

Every finite concept is of the carnal mind, a sense of selfhood or power apart from God; but with that acknowledgment, we go into the silence to realize that what is appearing as the mind of man or the "arm of flesh" is not power, is not presence, is not law.

We do not need to fear to look at the words "infection" and "contagion." We can look at them and realize:

You are of your father the devil, or nothingness, a product of the carnal mind, which is not mind and which has no law.

You are a nothingness because all that God made is good and anything God did not make was not made.

When we are back in oneness, not condemning and not judging, the Holy Ghost descends upon us. If a few of us are able to stand and look out at every man, woman, child, and thing everywhere on the globe and say, "Material power? That's atheistic. That's claiming a power apart from God. There is only one power, the power of the Spirit," miracles of Grace can happen.

Infinite Way groups could unite and decide that every day of the week they would spare one minute for the cause of peace, one minute to close their eyes, smile, and thank God that material power is atheism but that a reliance on the Spirit of God, the presence of God, the power of God, the word of God, this is truly power. Material power is nonpower, the "arm of flesh." Surely then peace would come, and quickly.

In a vision, I saw all the power of armaments as dead matter, saw it could not move itself because it had nobody to move it. How can anyone move anything if someone is standing facing him with the word of God as his consciousness?

Most of us know by experience that matter is not power, and most of us also know it is the word of God in the consciousness of the practitioner that is the power. Matter responds and turns from sick matter to healthy matter not by material application, not by the power of material force, but by the power of the Word entertained in consciousness.

This daily proving that the word of God in individual consciousness is sufficient to stop matter in its tracks and change sick matter into good matter, sick bodies

into well bodies, sick purses into healthy purses, unemployed people into employed people, and bring together harmonious relationships between capital and
labor has been going on for years.

Everything that represents material form or material
power—bombs, germs, or infections—is inactive, a
nothingness. It takes an individual to move it. But an
individual is free to do good or evil, except when faced
with the power of the Word. Then one loses all power
to do evil. That is why reforms have taken place
through truth awakening in the consciousness of an
individual. That is why healings of false desires, alcohol-
ism, and drug addiction have been brought about. The
dead matter—the alcohol and the drugs—has been
proved dead in the face of an individual who maintains
the word of God in the midst of him, in his consciousness.

The word of God removes fear because it brings to
light the truth that in the presence of that Word there is
no power. Nothing is power and nobody is power in the
presence of the realized word of God. If we human
beings just think about our personal affairs and give no
thought or little thought to the Word, then it cannot be
said we have the Lord God, because we do not.

This whole world would be safe and secure, this
whole world would be at peace if people kept the word
of God alive in their consciousness. Not by reading it,
not by hearing it will we be saved. By maintaining the
word of God, the promise of God in our consciousness
will harmony, peace, and health be brought forth into
expression in our experience. We are then no longer in
the tomb of humanhood. We have risen to the mystical
consciousness of Oneness.

~ 2 ~

RELEASING SPIRITUAL POWER

IN The Infinite Way, we have left behind the theological belief in a God-power that does things to error or evil, a God-power that fights the devil or fights sin or disease; and we have accepted as truth the mystical principle that Spirit is omniscient, omnipotent, and omnipresent, besides which there is nothing else. What we have to demonstrate, therefore, is that in the presence of spiritual power there are no powers of sin, disease, lack, accident, unhappiness, or any other type of human misery. These negative things can exist only in the absence of spiritual power.

Darkness can exist only in the absence of light. Spiritual power is often described as Light: the Light of the world, the Light that lights the way, the Light that lights our footsteps. Throughout all mystical literature, Light has been the symbol of spiritual presence and power. This Light never battles darkness. The Light that is the Christ never fights any form of discord.

Jesus never fought sin; he forgave it. He never fought disease, argued with it or against it. He said, "Arise, and take up thy bed, and walk."[1] There is only one record in the Bible of his resisting evil, and that is when he threw the "moneychangers" out of the temple.[2]

My personal belief is that was his way of telling his disciples we have to throw all negative and destructive qualities out of our consciousness. Consciousness is the temple. The negative, superstitious, evil, sensual, or lustful beliefs are the moneychangers. They represent the materialistic sense we must cast out of our consciousness.

Except for Jesus' encounter with the moneychangers, the Master taught, "Resist not evil."[3] "Put up again thy sword . . . for all they that take the sword shall perish with the sword."[4] The Light of the world does not argue with darkness, fight, or try in any way to remove darkness. The Light, being the Light, cannot be extinguished by any darkness.

"Where the Spirit of the Lord is, there is liberty."[5] It does not say, where the Spirit of the Lord is, "there is a battle," or where the Spirit of the Lord is, "there is a fight with error." On the contrary, where the Spirit of the Lord is, there is peace, there is liberty. "In thy presence is fulness of joy."[6] Certainly, this does not indicate battling or fighting or any sense of overcoming. Rather, it indicates that where God is realized, there is peace because there is nothing with which to contend. Light does not contend with darkness; and in the presence of light, there is no darkness, no sin, no disease, no death, no lack, no limitation, no unhappy human relationships. If we accept this as a principle, we will demonstrate spiritual power, the presence of God, and that is all. But the working out of this principle in our daily experience is an individual thing. There are no formulas; there is no possibility of laying down a specific way to demonstrate this.

The Master gave us the principle of nonresistance, but he did not show us how it is done. After we have the principle, it is up to us to see how to bring it forth in daily experience and prove that in the presence of this realized spiritual power, temporal power, whether of a material, mental, moral, or financial nature, is not a power. In fact, it does not even exist in the presence of that spiritual Light that we are.

THE UNKNOWN QUANTITY

"I have meat to eat that ye know not of."[7] This meat can be referred to as spiritual power: I have spiritual power. From this, it follows that we have dominion because God gave us this spiritual power, which is the dominion. So we have dominion; we have spiritual power the world knows not of. The world has no way at all of knowing even if there is such a thing as spiritual power or what spiritual power can do. The subject of spiritual power is an unknown quantity to the human mind. That is why Charles Steinmetz, the great scientist and electrical wizard, said the greatest discovery in the twentieth century would be the discovery of spiritual power. The human world is relying on temporal power. It is relying on bombs and missiles; it is placing its faith in one form or another of mental or physical power, all of which is temporal power. But we have been told to put up the sword and to resist not evil.

The Master further said, "Be not afraid."[8] Would the Master have told us not to fear if he had known about atomic power? I am sure he would have because he demonstrated he had discovered the secret of spiritual power. We know that in the presence of spiritual power, temporal powers are not power. We are proving it in some measure in the healing of disease, in the overcoming of sinful appetites and desires, and in overcoming lack, limitation, accidents, and the results of accidents; but this has been accomplished only in a small degree.

DISCOVERING THE NATURE OF SPIRITUAL POWER

When we remember that the principle of spiritual power was given to the world nearly twenty centuries ago, we cannot be too proud of what has been accomplished spiritually in this century. True, far more has been demonstrated during the past seventy-five years than in the previous nineteen hundred years; and that gives us hope and courage to go forward and realize that, even though we have not fully attained, at least we are on the pathway leading to the realization of the nature of spiritual power.

When we individually come to understand this, each one of us will be doing some measure of healing work for ourselves and others. We will be bringing a measure of peace, health, and happiness into the lives of others, but only in the degree we individually solve the mystery of spiritual power. If one individual realizes the nature of spiritual power, he or she can bring a degree of harmony to thousands of others; but it will only be a degree of harmony. No one can bring complete harmony to another. That is something we each must do by casting the moneychangers out of our own consciousness.

We all have moneychangers in our consciousness in the sense that we all have some lingering belief in two powers: in physical disease and physical health, moral disease and moral health, and financial disease and financial health. These are the moneychangers we cast out, not by fighting, "not by might, nor by power,"[9] but by realization. That realization comes by asking how we can bring spiritual power into our experience, into the experience of the world, into our household, into our community, into our business or professional office, and into our government.

The real question we have to ask ourselves is how great is our desire to know God, to know spiritual power and spiritual presence. To what degree are we hungering and thirsting for spiritual realization? We might put it this way: How serious is our problem? For those still doing well physically and financially, this question of knowing God can probably wait until next year, the year after, five years from now, or until they begin to turn grey. But for those of us who have problems of a sufficiently deep or serious nature, now is the time to seek an understanding of the nature of spiritual power and spiritual presence.

When we realize the nature of Spirit, we do not have to wonder what to do with It. We do not have to do anything with It at all; It does Its own work. Once we attain the presence of God, that Presence establishes harmony. Once we attain an understanding of the nature of spiritual power, we are the Light, and there is no darkness to be dispelled.

But how do we manifest or express spiritual Light and realize spiritual power? What is the nature of spiritual Light? What is the nature of spiritual wisdom? Attaining that wisdom, we have nothing further to do. We do not have to apply spiritual wisdom when we have it. "In thy presence is fulness of joy," fulness of

Light, and in this Light, there is no darkness. We never need concern ourselves with how to heal disease or how to overcome sin or lack. We have only one concern: to know God, to know the nature of spiritual presence and spiritual power, to bring this Light of the world into expression. Beyond that, we have nothing to do about sin, disease, lack, or limitation because in the consciousness of spiritual power these do not exist.

RISING ABOVE THE LEVEL OF THE PROBLEM

I recently received a letter telling me of a piece of real estate the owner wanted to sell, explaining how this sale would bless and benefit somebody. It immediately came to my mind that in the kingdom of God, there is no real estate. We cannot take a real estate problem to God because there is no real estate or real estate problem in God. Real estate cannot be sold by thinking of real estate. We cannot meet the problem on the level of the problem. We must recognize that if God knows nothing about real estate, it is none of our business. All we are called upon to do is to know God, to bring to light spiritual power in our consciousness.

When people have written to me about employment, it has come to me that in the kingdom of God there is no employment; there is no employer and there is no employee. Sometimes from a metaphysical standpoint, it has been said that God is both the employer and the employee; but in God, there is only Spirit. What we are doing is trying to patch up our concept of heaven, and heaven has no employer and it has no employees.

"My kingdom is not of this world."[10] "My* kingdom" does not include real estate or employment. "My kingdom" has in it the grace of God. Then what is "My

---

*The words "Me," " My," and "Mine," capitalized, refer to God.

kingdom" that is not of this world? That is a question to be answered from within our consciousness. All we know about the kingdom of God is that the New Testament says it is not of this world. All we know about spiritual peace is that this world cannot give it. If we think we are going to solve our problem and find our peace by selling real estate or getting employment, all we are doing is perpetuating ourselves in the human sense of life; whereas if we can discover within ourselves the nature of spiritual power, we have found the great secret of life.

There have always been different forms and different degrees of material power in the world, from the bow and arrow up to the atomic bomb. In the last century, there has arisen also the question of mental power and how to use it: how to exercise it to win friends, influence and control other people. But with spiritual power, we are dealing with a power unknown to the human mind because the human mind cannot understand or receive spiritual wisdom. "The natural man,"[11] the carnal mind, "is not subject to the law of God, neither indeed can be."[12]

The human mind cannot know the law of God. How then are you and I to know it? First, we have to stop thinking in terms of real estate, employment, fevers or germs, lack or abundance, disease or health, purity or sin, and all the things that apply to this world and to the human being, to the "creature."[13] We have to turn within: What is the nature of my Christ-identity? What is the nature of my Self created in the image and likeness of God?

THE NATURE OF SPIRITUAL SELFHOOD

None of us doubts for a minute that some part of us was made in the image and likeness of God. Some part of us must be divine; some part of us must be the spiritual child of God that receives the things of God and knows the Father face to face. There is some part of us that can say, "I live; yet not I"–I have spiritual presence and spiritual power–"Christ liveth in me."[14]

The task of each one of us is to turn within with the question: What is the nature of my spiritual selfhood? What is the nature of my sonship, my spiritual sonship, my divine sonship? What is the nature of the "me" that receives the things of God? What is the nature of the "me" that God created in His own image and likeness? What is the nature of the son of God, to whom the Father says, "Son, thou art ever with me, and all that I have is thine"?[15] God is not saying that to me as a human being because in my humanhood I do not have all God's blessings, supply, health, or harmony.

But there is a part of me that receives God's grace from everlasting to everlasting. God's love changes not; the things of God are forever. So as we search deep inside ourselves for the mystery of life, each one of us should go within asking, Who am I? What am I? Who am I in the image and likeness of God? What am I in the image and likeness of God? What am I as the child of God? What is there about me that is receiving God's grace from everlasting to everlasting, that has never been without it and will never be without it? What of me is the spiritual selfhood that is heir of God, that lives "not by might, nor by power," but by the Spirit of God that is in me? This is the nature of our searching and what it must be.

In the presence of the dominion that God gave us, there are no problems, nothing of sin, lack, or disease to be overcome. "Neither death, nor life . . . shall be able to separate us from the love of God."[16] From the standpoint of our humanhood, we have all been separated from the love of God. Then what is this Christ-self of us that can never be separated from the love of God, the life of God, the immortality of God, the infinite being of God? Let us set about discovering the nature of that Christ-self and the dominion God gave us in the beginning that has never been taken from us and that we still have in our spiritual identity.

Whatever measure of Christhood we can bring to light becomes a law of healing to persons turning to us. Whatever measure of spiritual dominion we can attain solves and dissolves their problems. Whatever measure of God's wisdom or grace can be revealed in us becomes a law of harmony and peace unto them. In the degree of their realization of their Christhood, they in turn become a law of harmony in their household and community. Eventually, their influence spreads further into the world in proportion to the degree of their realization of the nature of their spiritual selfhood, the nature of their spiritual dominion, and the nature of the spiritual Light they are.

If we can bring to light some measure of realization of our Christ-nature, our Christ-self, and some measure of realization of the spiritual dominion with which we were endowed in the beginning, we will be a tremendous influence in our community and in the entire world.

We are pioneers in the work of bringing the nature of spiritual power to bear on human affairs. As students of The Infinite Way, our major function is to learn the nature of spiritual power and then to bring it into actual experience on earth. When we first came to a spiritual or metaphysical way of life, our main object was to find solutions for our own problems. There is nothing wrong with this. This is the way it had to be because in finding a way to solve our own problems, we learned that we received enough of spiritual power to help others with their problems.

EVIDENCING SPIRITUAL POWER

A strange thing takes place at this stage of our unfoldment. We begin to see it is no longer necessary to work on our own problems because, first, we have so few of them and, second, our problems have a way of disappearing without any personal thought about them; so our life eventually is spent in a ministry for others. In forsaking our own problems and in devoting ourselves to others, we no longer have problems; and the few that come are quickly solved. This is a principle of life.

We can go a step further and discover that behind this principle there is a still greater one: our needs are met in proportion to our giving. Our spiritual giving is the very substance and activity of our supply. The more we give, the more we have; the more we exercise our dominion, the more dominion we have. This spiritual principle operates at every level of our existence.

Into this there enters a still greater principle: the more we are in the consciousness of giving, the less evidence of self there is. We soon learn, too, that the total elimination of our problems comes with the elimination of our little self, that selfhood apart from God, that personal selfhood. In giving this up, we attain the awareness of our real Self.

If you should ask me for help, I would be thinking in terms of spiritual presence, spiritual power, divine wisdom, and divine life. Into my consciousness would come the truth that God constitutes individual being: God constitutes your mind, your life, your soul; God is the law unto your being; God is the lawgiver. God is the activity unto your experience; and because God is infinite, no other power can stand as power. All other powers dissolve in the light of the Light.

By the very nature of the son of God, there must be an absence of sin, death, lack, and limitation. The son of God raised up is the Light of the world. Therefore, if the son of God is realized here and now, the Light of the world is recognized here and now; and in this recognition of the Light, the calls for help would be met, and freedom would be made manifest. Even though we would have given no thought to ourselves in any part of this prayer, meditation, or treatment, if the Christ is realized, our own problems would have to disappear at the same instant theirs did because we would both be included in that Light. We could not manifest the Light and be separate from It ourselves.

REALIZING THE PRESENCE OF GOD
AS OMNIPRESENCE

As we recognize Omnipresence, that is, the presence of all spiritual knowledge and wisdom, we recognize that it cannot be confined to a room or a place. Our realized Christ has a way of seeping through the cracks, going through the wall just as the Master did. When we declare Omniscience, that is, infinite spiritual wisdom, we are not talking merely about your wisdom or mine: we are talking about Omniscience, all Wisdom, and that would have to be the wisdom of all persons throughout our city, community, nation, and even the world.

When we are in prayer or meditation, we are not realizing the presence of God in us, but Omnipresence, All-presence, everywhere equally. In this way, we can lose sight of our personal selfhood in the recognition of our divine Selfhood, which is the Selfhood of every individual; and thus we can bring that divine Selfhood around us. Then everywhere there is greater evidence of a divine Wisdom, a divine Power, a divine Presence, even though most persons might not know why, how, or wherefore.

There is a spiritual reason for this, which is important to understand. Everyone on the face of the earth without exception is seeking God or a knowledge of God. It makes no difference how a person would speak of that search, even if it were negatively by saying there is no God. But that would be like some persons who whistle when they walk through graveyards. They whistle because they are trying to convince themselves there are no ghosts; but by whistling, they are evidencing their fear of or their belief in them. One reason atheists deny God is they believe there is a God they do not want to face.

Disregarding our atheistic friends for the moment, whether a person is a Catholic, a Protestant, a Jew, a Vedantist, or a follower of any other religion, there is a seeking, an urge, a drive within to know and to find God. If nothing else, there is a hope that God may reveal Himself or be made evident. It is this secret longing in the heart that makes every individual responsive to prayer or meditation wherever it is going on. In his heart, he is longing for some divine guidance as to what is right, what is necessary, or what lies ahead. Everyone is craving some knowledge greater than his own, some wisdom greater than his education or experience has given him. As long as this drive is in an individual, he is praying; and as long as he is praying, there will be an answer to his prayer.

Our prayer for peace is a prayer for spiritual guidance. As long as we are reaching out for something greater than ourselves, we will receive guidance. But while we are receiving guidance, our own problems will have disappeared because the nature of them was illusion to begin with; and our ability to ignore them and turn to the spiritual realities gave that nothingness a chance to dissolve into the nothingness it is. It is only while we are treating problems that we perpetuate them. That is why in our work we turn away from the problem to the attainment of spiritual awareness, that is, the inner realization of spiritual identity, spiritual law, and spiritual life. Then when we open our eyes, the problem is gone or is on the way out.

At this stage of our spiritual development, while we still want to see our individual sins and diseases and lacks disappear, at least we know they are going to disappear only in proportion as we can take our attention away from them and begin to realize the omnipresence of infinite Grace. There is no such thing as a divine Grace that operates for you or for me. Divine Grace is infinite in its nature, and it operates for the children of God universally. When a person asks why this Grace withholds something from him, it is because he is not attuned to It and does not understand the universal nature of Grace.

THE ULTIMATE GOAL OF THE REVELATION OF SPIRITUAL POWER

When we begin to pray for our children, our family, or our neighbors; when we hear, see, or read about men and women gathering together for some national or international purpose; or when we pray for the realization of Omnipresence, Omnipotence, and Omniscience, we are praying for the freedom of this world. But because we are in the world, our prayers will bring our freedom, too. Let us not think we can pray for our freedom, leave the world out, and have our prayers answered; we cannot pray for God's sun to shine in our garden alone. We must pray that the sun shines, and let it shine on our friend's and our enemy's gardens. We cannot pray to God for a solution to our problems and leave all the rest out. There is no God listening to such prayers.

God is love. God does not love anyone separate and apart from all the rest. When we realize God's love, we realize it for each other. Even if we could heal one person here and one person there of cancer, what really is the final use unless through the revelation of spiritual power we can make cancer disappear off the face of the earth? How insignificant an individual life would be if it could attain complete harmony without consideration for the rest of mankind!

How great is one individual life dedicated to the realization of Omnipotence, Omniscience, and Omnipresence. With that realization, storms could be made to disappear and not return because storms are not a phenomenon of nature as it is scientifically believed. Storms are phenomena of human consciousness. Where human consciousness is at peace, storms do not appear. We can test this in our homes. If we find our peace within, storms in the home and in the family disappear. It is only necessary for one individual in a household to find inner peace to change the entire household.

Eventually, disease will disappear from the face of the earth. Up to this time, when a cure for one disease has been found medically, another disease has usually come along to take its place. This is because disease cannot be eliminated from human consciousness because human consciousness believes in two powers, and it must always demonstrate its belief. As long as we believe in good and evil, we will have periods of good and periods of evil. As long as human consciousness is indulging hate, jealousy, or animosity, it manifests in some form of disease. If it is cured in one form, it will break out in another form because the cause is human consciousness and its belief in two powers.

PURIFYING OUR STATE OF CONSCIOUSNESS

Disease is healed when consciousness is purified, and this is true individually and collectively. When we permit our consciousness to be attuned or aligned with spiritual power, disease, sin, fear, and lack are eliminated from our consciousness. We cannot pray to God to bring spiritual power to remove our problem while the cause of the problem remains, and the cause is always human consciousness. Therefore, we must lift our consciousness up to the Divine. "I, if I be lifted

up,"[17] if we lift up the *I*, * if we lift up our consciousness
to divine sonship and let the spiritual Light touch our
consciousness and free us of hate, animosity, fear, and
jealousy, we will find no disease left, no lack left, no fear
left. All our work then is to attune our consciousness to
the Divine, opening ourselves to the realization of
Omnipresence, Omnipotence, and Omniscience,
praying from the heart: Thy will be done in me, not
mine.

Then we must give up any of the concepts we have
been entertaining: concepts of each other, concepts of
the world, concepts of all humanity. For example, you
and I as human beings have entertained concepts of
other peoples, other races, other nations, all of which
were false. We did not know it at the time, but most of
us know it now. Prejudice was rampant before World
War I. There were color prejudice, religious prejudice,
and political ideologies that caused people to war with
each other. These ideologies were not necessarily right
or wrong, but prejudice resulted from the motives we
ascribed to those who held them.

We must eliminate from our consciousness the hate,
the fear, and the distrust through knowing they represent merely our false concepts of one another. When we
are willing to drop these and recognize that at the center
of being each of us is the same child of God, we will
attune ourselves to spiritual principles; and healings will
begin to flow. We do not have to ask God to heal us.
There have been millions of people who have died
while praying, asking God to heal them. All we need to
do is begin to love our neighbor as ourselves and

---

*The word *I*, italicized, refers to God.

thereby bring ourselves into harmony with the laws of God so that the laws of God can function.

The laws of God cannot function in a consciousness filled with false concepts. We must attune ourselves to the Divine. If we look at persons and see all their human differences, before long we will like some and dislike others; we are going to trust some and distrust others. We will have so many differences that our own minds will be confused.

If, however, we can recognize that, regardless of appearances, Divinity is the nature of every person's being and that God made us in His own image and likeness, we are knowing the truth about all persons. Whether one is acting it out here on earth or not is none of our business; and if we are aware of any sin in another, instead of sitting in judgment, we should inwardly practice the New Testament principle: "Judge not, that ye be not judged."[18]

Therefore, we will not judge: we will take the attitude: "Father, forgive them; for they know not what they do."[19] We are realizing that every person is a branch of the same tree, the Tree of Life. In that, there is no judgment, no criticism. There is forgiveness "seventy times seven,"[20] forgiveness and a praying that their eyes be opened. This is attuning ourselves to the Divine, making ourselves receptive to divine healing, to divine Grace, to divine protection because we have wiped out our human concepts of persons and are seeing them as the image and likeness of God, seeing them spiritually as the very Christ of God. We are not using our human judgment; we are using our spiritual intuition to recognize that God made all of us in His own image and likeness and looked on us and found us good.

There is nothing in us of criticism, of condemnation, of judgment; and, therefore, our consciousness is open to receive the grace of God. If we believe there are two powers, we are setting up a barrier in our own consciousness. If, however, we are realizing Omnipotence, Omniscience, and Omnipresence, we are again attuning ourselves to the exercise of spiritual power, spiritual wisdom.

In the proportion we bring ourselves into oneness with the principles set forth in the Master's teaching, our consciousness is imbued with spiritual power from on High. We credit Christ Jesus with being the most illumined soul who ever walked the earth because we have never heard or read of any evil sense in his nature. He was endowed from on High with spiritual power because he had that degree of consciousness prepared to receive it. He held within himself no criticism, no judgment, no antagonism, no desire to avail himself of temporal power. He had within him no desire to see anyone punished, regardless of the offense. In other words, his was a pure consciousness. Therefore, it could be the transparency for the presence and power of God.

The Master commands us to go and do likewise, but we cannot be endowed with spiritual power while we present ourselves to this world with a carnal mind. It is only in the degree that we can pray for each other, friend and enemy; it is only in the degree that we can realize Omnipotence, Omniscience, and Omnipresence universally that our problems are dissolved and our consciousness becomes a transparency for spiritual power that enables us to heal, reform, forgive, and supply others.

Until we can bring ourselves to that place where we are willing not only to heal but to feed and clothe multitudes, until we are willing to be used for spreading this supply of dollars or whatnot, we are not opening our consciousness to spiritual endowment because the spiritually endowed do not receive: they are the instrumentalities through which God's grace is given. While we are praying to receive, we are blocking spiritual power.

When we are praying, "Father, I am willing to heal and feed the multitudes. Just let Your grace flow," we will find It flowing. What a mistake has been the belief that we could pray to get something for ourselves when actually we can receive only when we are praying in order to give, share, and multiply. The result of that selfish praying is that we have built up an ego, a personal sense, and then wanted God to increase it. God does not increase your personal fortune or mine as long as we want Him to do this. It is only when we begin the pouring out of even the little that we have that our own increases beyond any possible measure of our own needs.

In this age, spiritual power and the nature of its working have been discovered. As we continue to learn more and more about spiritual power, we will prepare ourselves to be worthy instruments for its flow—not so much for your good or mine but that the entire world may be embraced in divine Love. Then you and I will partake of it because we are part of that world.

~ 3 ~

SPIRITUAL POWER UNVEILED

WHEN people reach a point of desperation, their ears once again are attuned to hear the Word within and their eyes are opened to spiritual power. In a period of temporal prosperity and temporal might, these are forgotten. Very little thought is given to the fact that in every age faith has been placed in material or temporal powers. It must be surprising to those who rely wholly on material power to read the history of the Pharaohs and to realize the Hebrew people, without arms, ammunition, army, or financial resources, broke away from their rulers, who had the gold and silver, the soldiers, the horses, and the armaments. Without weapons, storehouses, barns, or any sign of temporal power, the Master lifted his people above the authority of the Caesars and revealed to them the nature of true freedom and abundance.

Since that time, we have seen the rise of many ruthless dictators and powerful armies and navies; and there have been great concentrations of power and wealth in a few nations. Certainly, it would seem with all this there would be no end to their reign, but we have only to read history to see how all this has tumbled and been made nothing. Always there comes a time when temporal power fails, when the mightiest fall, and when those from whom it would appear there is no escape prove their weakness. Who would have believed the Russian people could ever become free of their czars? Such a thing must have been unthinkable with all the armies, power, and wealth the czars had. And yet, in a short span, that power was gone.

A FEAR-RIDDEN WORLD

Today we seem to have forgotten history. We have permitted ourselves to experience fear and doubt, doubt that we will survive or that freedom will survive. Whatever we have of temporal power, we are afraid to trust; and whatever of temporal power someone else has, we are being made to fear. This is because we have forgotten that temporal power never is a power when spiritual power is on the scene. We have completely forgotten the three-year ministry of Christ Jesus, in which he faced every type of temptation, every type of power, and proved its nothingness. Sin was proved nothing in his presence; disease was proved nothing in his presence; death itself was overcome. He almost laughed when Pilate said, "Knowest thou not that I have power to crucify thee, and have power to release thee? Jesus answered, Thou couldest have no power at all against me, except it were given thee from above."[1]

People all over the world today are filled with anxiety. I am not speaking alone of the threat of foreign dictatorships. That is but one facet of the danger today. For some, the major threat is peace because in peacetime the question arises as to how to keep people employed, the economy on the upswing, and the payrolls met. All this brings the fear of a depression because peace has problems, too, with billions of dollars not spent for armaments and billions of dollars of payrolls not in existence. Furthermore, there is always some new, more deadly disease to be concerned about. On every side, we are threatened by either temporal power or its failure; but when all these temporal powers are threatening to engulf us is the time to remember not only that spiritual power operates but how it operates.

From the time of Christ Jesus, there has been little evidence that anyone had any knowledge of spiritual power. In fact, since that time, spiritual power, to all intents and purposes, has not been in operation in our world. Its secret was lost a few centuries after the Master. Ours, however, is the century in which spiritual power is to be revealed.

THE NATURE OF SPIRITUAL POWER

To know the nature of spiritual power, we must practice it. Talking about water will not quench thirst; we must drink it. Talking about food will never satisfy the stomach; we must eat it. So it is with spiritual power. It can be described to us, but that will not make it operate in our experience. To learn its nature and operation, we must embody it, practice it, and bring it into our experience.

In the materialistic state of consciousness, we know and understand matter and material values, material forces and powers; but Christ Jesus, who brought the world the Christian message, proved there is another dimension. When he said, "My peace I give unto you: not as the world giveth, give I unto you,"[2] he was speaking of a peace that comes from another dimension. In his statement, "My kingdom is not of this world,"[3] it is plain the Christ-kingdom does not consist of more chariots, more horses, more airplanes, more armaments, more gold, and more silver. "My kingdom is not of this world," and yet "My kingdom" overcomes "this world," without battleships, without bombs, and without the weapons of temporal power.

The religious world had been trying for centuries to get the power of Spirit to do something to the power of matter. But it has not brought peace on earth; it has not wiped out the armaments of the world and turned them into "pruning hooks."[4] We have made a mistake: spiritual power is not to be used to overcome material power. The power of Spirit is not to be used to overcome the power of matter; the power of God is not to be used to overcome the sins or diseases of the world.

The nature of spiritual power is omnipotence; and the only way we can bring spiritual power into our life is to look at any phase of material power–discord, inharmony, lack, or disease–and realize, "You are not power! Thou couldest have no power at all against me, except it were given thee from above!"

The Master did not call down the power of Spirit to still a storm, he merely said, "Peace, be still."[5] God is not in the whirlwind; God is not in matter; God is not in material force or powers; God is not in the temporalities. God is Spirit; and besides Him, there are no powers.

We have proved this in many phases of life. Tens of thousands have been healed in this century, not by using the power of God to stop a disease, not by calling upon the Spirit to overcome material conditions, but by quietly realizing that besides God, there is no power. We have witnessed this in business relationships—never by fighting, never by carrying on a campaign, but always in the same way, quietly, peacefully realizing, "Besides God, there is none else."

We have tried to reach God to get God to do something to something that had no power. We have tried to use Truth. This we cannot do. We do not use Truth; we do not use God. That would be making God a servant. God is not our servant. God is not to be used. God is to be understood. Truth is not to be used. Truth is to be understood.

THE FOLLY OF FIGHTING TEMPORAL POWER

The Master wiped out disease, death, and sin. It is the will of God that we be whole, complete, perfect, eternal, immortal, sinless, and pure. We aren't because instead of realizing that the very nature of God is omnipresence and omnipotence and resting quietly and peacefully in that truth, we have been looking for a God to do something, as if God could do something today or tomorrow that he was not doing yesterday. If God could have overcome our particular problem, he would have done it because it is God's will that we live. "For I have no pleasure in the death of him that dieth, saith the Lord God: wherefore turn yourselves, and live ye."[6] "For I came down from heaven, not to do mine own will, but the will of him that sent me."[7]

God is the same yesterday, today, and forever, from everlasting to everlasting. We cannot influence God to do something tomorrow. Two times two has always been four: even God cannot change that tomorrow.

That has been from everlasting to everlasting, and it will be forever.

There has never been a time when the Christ was not enthroned in our consciousness. "Before Abraham was, I am."[8] "Lo, I am with you alway, even unto the end of the world."[9] We look for a power, a God-power, a Christ-power; and here it is. The secret of spiritual power is as simple as that. In saying, "Resist not evil,"[10] Jesus did not mean for us to be eaten up by it. He was recognizing the truth that evil is not the power it seems to be. When he said, "Put up again thy sword . . . for all they that take the sword shall perish with the sword,"[11] he did not mean, "Put it up until 1980, and then take out that sword. He spoke of the sword in the sense of temporal power. It makes no difference whether it is a sword or a bomb, whether it is a great deal of gold or a little gold. He is talking about putting up temporal power, resisting not evil, stopping fighting the devil, and learning the devil is not power. Why fight carnal mind or mortal mind? They are not power. God is Spirit and God is omnipotence; therefore, Spirit is omnipotence, all powerful.

We can prove this. It may take a day, a week, or a month because we have been accustomed to looking for powers with which to do something. Before this century, it was material power. Although we still look for material power, in this century we have also been searching for mental and spiritual powers. There is spiritual power, but it does not do anything because "As birds flying, so will the Lord of hosts defend Jerusalem; defending also he will deliver it; and passing over he will preserve it."[12]

This spiritual power creates, maintains, and sustains; but if we can be made to accept the belief in two powers, the trouble begins. It began that way for Adam. Adam really knew the truth, that there is only one power, and was very happy in that knowledge; but then he ate of the tree of the knowledge of good and evil, two powers. The moment he did, he had to look around for a God to do something to the evil power. We have been doing that ever since, living the Adamic life, always looking for a power to do something to the evils that plague us, even though these evils are not power except in our acceptance of them as power.

We have been afraid of mortals and what they could do to us. We have placed our faith in everything from tomahawks to atomic bombs. When the atomic bomb was discovered and used, it would seem that we had reached the ultimate of power and never again would there be any more trouble on earth. But the more power we strive for, the more power is necessary to overcome it; and then the more power it will take to overcome that. It is similar to drugs. A person begins by taking a small amount, but the quantity is continuously increased because the more one takes, the more one needs the next time.

PROVING SPIRITUAL POWER IS THE ALL-POWER

Because for many centuries we have feared so many different kinds of powers, feared even the power of silver and gold, it may take a week, two, three, or four to discipline ourselves to be able to look out at any and every form of error we have feared—sin, disease, or bombs—and realize, "Father, forgive me; I did not know what I was doing." With the whole ministry of Christ Jesus, with two thousand years of his word, how can it be that we do not believe we have the Lord God Almighty?

As long as we seek to use spiritual power on anything or anybody, we will never be able to prove its truth. The secret of spiritual power is in the realization that it is the all-power, and there are no other powers. Let us begin with simple things, something that does not frighten us, and lead up gradually to the more serious things of life and are able to prove, by our refraining from the use of power, even the attempt to use God-power, that there are no powers out here.

This is the revelation of the nature of spiritual power as given to me, based on thirty years of demonstrating and proving that evil is not a power. It is a power only while an individual accepts two powers. When an individual accepts the Christ-message, "Resist not evil," the nothingness of error is proved, regardless of what form it takes. It rests with us as individuals.

We cannot go through our whole life living on someone else's demonstration. Sooner or later, our lack of realization, if it continues, will catch up with us. We must consciously remind ourselves, "From now on, I am accepting a God within me, so that 'if I ascend up into heaven,' or 'if I make my bed in hell,'[13] this God will be with me. If I go through the 'valley of the shadow of death,'[14] this God will go with me because this God is within me. The whole kingdom of God is within me." We must do this consciously.

The next step is to acknowledge consciously that God is almighty—the all-might, the all-power, Spirit. We cannot see Spirit, hear It, taste It, touch It, or smell It. We have to understand that It is, even though we do not have physical proof of It. We have to have enough spiritual discernment to feel within ourselves that this is true, and then we have to learn to look out at the things we have feared and begin consciously to realize, "How foolish. The All-might is within me. Spirit is the all-might, and I have feared 'man, whose breath is in his nostrils.'[15] I have feared alcohol; I have feared disease; I have feared false appetite; I have feared atheism; I have feared communism; I have even feared capitalism."

What difference does it make what we fear? Whatever it is, when we fear, we are acknowledging a power other than God. We are acknowledging two powers; and when we have two powers, we are cast out of the Garden of Eden and we have to earn our living by the sweat of our brow, bring forth children in pain, and learn how to be go-getters, because with two powers we are always looking for one power to do something to the other. But when we acknowledge God as Spirit and Spirit as the infinite All-power, we are no longer looking for a power.

THE OPEN SESAME

"Look upon Zion, the city of our solemnities: thine eyes shall see Jerusalem a quiet habitation, a tabernacle that shall not be taken down; not one of the stakes thereof shall ever be removed, neither shall any of the cords thereof be broken . . . And the inhabitant shall not say, I am sick: the people that dwell therein shall be forgiven their iniquity."[16] The evils are forgiven those who dwell in the consciousness of the presence of an almighty Spirit, forgiven in the sense of being erased and forgotten. In other words, healing really means being forgiven. To be healed of our diseases is really to be forgiven the sin of duality, forgiven the sin of believing there are two powers and that God is not almighty power. We are really being forgiven the acceptance of the belief that there is a power other than God. The way to experience that healing is to stop fighting the condition, stop fearing "man, whose breath is in his nostrils," stop fearing the boaster, the braggart, stop fearing the rattling of weapons. They are meant only to frighten us, but we cannot be frightened if we have an almighty God.

How is it possible for a God-loving people ever to fear godlessness or any of its work? Godlessness is not a power. There is no use pretending there is a God we believe in if we also believe godlessness is a power.

No one ever has a chance to defeat God or the godly. We will dwell in quiet and peaceful habitations when we learn, as Ralph Waldo Emerson said, that the dice of God are always loaded. No one has a chance against God, against Spirit, against love, freedom, and justice. No one has a chance against the spiritually minded. Even disease cannot take root in the spiritually minded. It can come close to them and threaten them; but all they need do is look out at it and realize, "We have the Lord God Almighty," turn over and go to sleep, and *let* there be light, *let* there be freedom, *let* it be revealed on earth that there is God. Then even the godless will behold the works of God and see that God and only God is mighty.

God in the midst of us already knows what is to be done, and it is His good pleasure to give us the kingdom, to give us freedom, to give us joy, to give us abundance. Give, give! The word is always "give," but we have to be quiet and confident enough to receive.

Once we catch such a glimpse of God, we will have caught the meaning of spiritual power. Let it be our password, our open sesame. Let it be what opens all doors for us—spiritual power. We do not try to get it; we do not try to use it; we do try to apply it: we just realize it and relax in it. We are not resisting evil; nevertheless, evil will flee. It will dissolve. In some normal, natural way, harmony will come into being.

OVERCOMING THE WORLD

The type of warfare that could embroil the world today can never result in a victory for anybody. Therefore no one in his right mind is going to start any of the wars that threaten us. The protection that is necessary is not more or better bombs. I am not a pacifist and am not trying to stop anyone from manufacturing bombs. But the world will be saved by spiritual power alone, and spiritual power comes only through the consciousness of individuals. There has always been spiritual power; but until it comes through a Moses, an Elijah, a Jesus, a Paul, or anyone else who attains this understanding, it is not in evidence. Spiritual power will govern this earth through our individual consciousness in proportion to our not fearing the error and not using spiritual power against the error, just declaring within ourselves "Spiritual power."

Someday we will have a body of people in this world touched by the Spirit; they will meet; and peace will be. Peace will come through the activity of the Spirit that is now abroad in the world, touching people of all lands. Those who have been touched by the Spirit are helping and can further help to awaken humanity to this touch of the Spirit by their prayers, by fulfilling acts of Grace–forgiveness, praying for the enemy–but above all, by an understanding of the nature of the Messiah. The Messiah taught, "My kingdom is not of this world."[17] "Put up again thy sword into his place: for all they that take the sword shall perish with the sword."[18]

Most people think of God as an almighty King; they even sing hymns to the almighty King, the King that goes out before them to slay their enemies, the King that conquers lands for them. The result has been that when conquerors have gone out with armies, there has always been a minister or priest to bless them, as if God sanctioned or could bless the conquering of other peoples. Armies and navies go out to slay, and somebody can always be found to say a prayer for them.

All this is based on the erroneous ancient Hebrew teaching that God is an almighty King and that His function is to see that our enemies are slain and that we are victorious. We must always be victorious, which would be true if only we could be victorious as the Master taught: "I have overcome the world."[19] He overcame not the world of Caesar, not the world outside. What he really meant was, "I have overcome the world in *me;* I have overcome greed, lust, mad ambition; I have overcome sensuality, false desires, false appetites. I have overcome 'this world' in me."

Even when spiritually we have overcome the world, a ruthless dictator may be sitting in the seat of power or the bomb may still be out there. Nevertheless, it will be true that we have overcome the world because we will have no fear of the bomb or the dictator; we will have no fear of sin or disease; we will have no fear of temptation; we will have no fear of lack or limitation. We have overcome the world because we have been touched by the Messiah, and the son of God has been lifted up in us. After we have been thus touched, we can say, "I live; yet not I, but Christ liveth in me."[20] "I can do all things through Christ which strengtheneth me."[21] When the Christ that dwelleth in us has been raised up, there is no need to take thought for our life because this son of God raised up in us goes before us to perform every function of our existence.

God is Spirit and must be worshiped in spirit and in truth. God is Spirit, and God governs through love, not by destroying anything but by the mystical revelation of the nonexistence of anything other than the presence of God. When we pray, let us not pray that God do anything but that the son of God be lifted up in us and govern our experience. We do not ask the Messiah to defeat our enemies or our competitors; we pray the Messiah be raised up in us as a spirit of love, and it will be so unto us. The more we dwell in the realization of God and the Christ as Spirit, the greater will be our own demonstration of the Christ in our experience.

The danger is in going back to the ancient beliefs that God or the Christ is some kind of a power and that once we get hold of It, we will be able to out-Houdini Houdini. Be assured we will not. We will not overcome any enemies; we will not overcome any competitors; we will just live, and move, and have our being in a joyous peace, abundance, and friendliness. We will live by Grace rather than by might or by power. All things are accomplished by the Spirit, not by might, not by power. It is a gentle Spirit. God is not in the whirlwind; God is not in sin, disease, or false appetites. God is not in poverty; God is in the "still small Voice."[22] To bring ourselves to a life under God means to bring ourselves to a life whereby we can be so still inwardly that when the still small Voice talks to us, it seems as if It were thundering.

Function of the Christ

The Christ is not something outside us that has to be sought. The Christ is something already within us, waiting to catch our attention.

What is the Christ? What is this Spirit of God in man? What is the function of the Christ in my life? What is the nature of the Presence that goes before me to make my way straight? What is the nature of the Power that appeared to Moses as "a cloud," "a pillar of fire," [23] and "manna" [24] falling from the sky? What is the nature of the Father within me that healed the sick for the Master? What is the nature of this Christ that is within me that enables me to forgive sinners?

What is the nature of this Christ that is the bread, the meat, the wine, and the water unto me, the woman at the well, and anyone who wishes to come to me?

Meditating along that line, the answer will come from within our being, but we must open the way.

This Christ, this Messiah, is within us. The Messiah is not a man who is going to come or a man who is going to come a second time. This Christ, this Messiah, is the Spirit of God that was planted in us in the beginning—not in the beginning of our parenthesis on earth but in the beginning when we were one with God, in the beginning when we were formed as the image and likeness of God. Its function is to live our life, to raise us up, to redeem us, to prepare paths for us, and to prepare mansions for us. It was given to us in the beginning. It is now locked up, and we must open a way so It can flow into our experience.

When the Spirit of God is upon us, we have awakened to the mystical consciousness. We are ordained and become aware that the son of God is in the midst of us:

There is within me an indwelling Something, a Presence, a Glory. It is not here to glorify me: Its function is to glorify God, to prove what life is when it is governed, maintained, and sustained by God.

Then we become witnesses to God's grace, to the presence of the Christ within us.

Only let us be careful we do not make of the Christ some kind of temporal power to help us acquire temporal things. Let us be satisfied that the Christ is the Spirit in us and that we can do all things through that Christ, with love, wisdom, judgment, equity, mercy, equality, and peace. The realization of this, and this alone, brings about "the peace which passeth all understanding."[25] There is no way to get peace from this world. We may attain fame and wealth and have more troubles than we bargained for. But the Master points out the difference: "My peace I give unto you: not as the world giveth."

We do not know humanly, and no one can tell us, what the nature of that peace is. *My* peace is the state of peace that descends upon us, not because of some good thing that happened in the outer world but because of some wonderful thing that took place within us. It is an assurance, "*I* am with you. *I* will never leave you; *I* will be with you to the end of the world." We could almost sing our way through life with that refrain once we have become aware that the Christ dwells in us. Now there is no need to worry, no need to fear. There is an invisible Presence making our path straight.

Peace on earth will not be attained by human efforts alone. Peace on earth is a gift of God that must be received by persons within the temple of their own being.

We can know by our own peaceableness, by our own inability to war with one another, to what degree the Christ has entered our Soul, to what degree we have received the gift of God, His son. The Christ raised up in the midst of us is the gift of God. If we have not yet received It in sufficient degree, it is still possible. The way is within us. The way is introspection, meditation, inner communion, and recognition that the son of God dwells in us and is ready at all times to speak to us. In fact, It is speaking to us even when we do not hear It. It has been thundering down at us through the ages.

It is the word of God by which we live—not by bread, not by money. It is by the word of God, which becomes flesh, that we are fed, clothed, and housed. It is by the word of God that a divine Grace takes over and makes us live at peace. It is this gift of God within the temple of our own being that establishes our peace with our fellow man: friends or enemies, near or far. It is the grace of God in our heart, the Christ that enters our Soul, that is the peace between us. Nothing else can give it to us; nothing else can maintain it. We can never find our support or our immortality in any other way than by this inner communion by means of which we hear the still small voice uttering the word of God.

"As birds flying," we will let the Spirit do Its work. *Let* It do Its work; *let* God. *Let* there be light; and we behold there is light. *Let* there be a firmament, and we behold there is a firmament. Let us behold God at work and resist the temptation to look for a power to use, to look for a truth to use, or to look for anything to use. Instead we relax in the assurance that God is Spirit, and this Spirit has promised It will never leave us or forsake us. It has always been with us, but we have neglected It. We not only neglected It, we have not known Its nature was Omnipotence; so we have tried to use It against something. There is nothing to use It against. Whatever seems evil to us is an appearance, and we have no right to judge by appearances. We must stop fighting error, stop trying to overcome it, stop looking for a God to overcome it, and acknowledge "God in the midst of me is almighty." Then we shall see the nature of spiritual power, as the silence reveals the Word made flesh.

PART II.

THE WORD
MADE FLESH

~4~

FLESH AND FLESH

THERE are very few scriptural quotations or passages of spiritual wisdom that do not have a double meaning, the literal and the intuitive, spiritual, or mystical. Many words and statements in the Bible seem contradictory, although I doubt there is a real contradiction in the entire Bible. There may seem to be contradictions if statements are interpreted from the concept a person has of the word or even from the definition of the word the dictionary gives, but I have not come across any.

Probably the most controversial word in Scripture is the word *flesh*, because in the Bible this word is used in two entirely different ways. Spirit, which is the original substance, is one form. It is the idea; and as it comes to us in our consciousness, it is the Word made flesh. When it becomes visible, it is the flesh that withers, the flesh we can enjoy today. But let us not hold on to the form tomorrow. Let us change our concept of being, body, or supply every day. Isaiah said, "All flesh is grass."[1] Jesus said, "The flesh profiteth nothing." [2] In the first chapter of John, it says, "And the Word was made flesh."[3]

"The Word was made flesh" may be considered one of the major premises in the Master's teaching, just as it is a major premise in the teaching of The Infinite Way. The word of God within us becomes visible or tangible as expression: the Word becomes the son of God. In that sense, flesh must be taken as meaning spiritual form, activity, and reality. "The Word was made flesh, and dwelt among us": God became visible as man. God the Father became visible as the son, but no one will ever see that man with his eyes. That man we can behold only at the height of spiritual awareness.

THE INVISIBLE WORD BECOMES TANGIBLE

Spiritual healers bring out healing only in that second they behold spiritual man: the Word made flesh. Up to that moment of realization, meditation or treatment is only leading them to where the Word becomes flesh as spiritual man.

A person can engage in healing meditations from morning until night, but if the meditation does not culminate in a split second of release—a freedom, joy, and peace—there is no use expecting a healing or the restoration of harmony from that meditation because it is not the thoughts a person thinks that bring out the healing. They only lead one up to a state of consciousness above the human sense of life wherein, in a moment of awareness, it is as if something flashes before the eyes and says, "Whereas I was blind, now I see."[4] And, of course, he may not have seen anything or heard anything and yet he knows, he perceives, he envisions.

As a person takes a statement of truth into his consciousness, ponders it, and finally stops pondering and just sits quietly with the ear open in expectation of something unfolding from within, that second of illumination comes—a flash, a release, a peace—and it is as if the person were released from his own body. There is a feeling of lightness, a feeling of joy, a feeling that it is done. It is in that second that he has become aware of Reality, the invisible God made tangibly manifest, even though he cannot see It with the eye or hear It with the ear.

After that, the fever may go down, the lump may be removed, supply may unfold, a job may be offered, or a new home may be found. All are the results in human experience of the invisible Word becoming tangible as an invisible feeling. First comes the invisible Word, God, the Infinite Invisible Itself, which we know is here and which is now filling all space within us and without us. Then follows the conscious realization of that Word being made evident in catching a glimpse of the Divine and finally out here in what we call the healing or a change in the appearance. But no appearance can change unless something has taken place in consciousness.

Do not watch appearances. Do not look for appearances to change. "Yet in my flesh shall I see God."[5] Right here and now on earth, we can see God. I do not mean we see with the physical eyes, but we can discern God or become aware of God. This is what is meant by seeing or feeling God: being touched by God or touching the hem of the Robe.

Every spiritual practitioner has received direct illumination, if in no other way than in the healing for which he was the instrument. Otherwise healing could not have taken place. There is nobody on earth today doing any greater works than the Master, Christ Jesus; and he said, "I can of mine own self do nothing."[6] I am sure we can do no more than he could. The Father within us does the work, but only in that moment of contact, of illumination. From then on, after one has had the illumination, that flow continues without conscious effort. But it must be renewed day by day. Every day it is necessary to go into the silence, sometimes a dozen times, to feel again that divine Impulse.

After one has been on this path several years, it is not necessary to go back and establish that contact with every meditation or treatment given. There comes a time when "we live, and move, and have our being"[7] in God; and we are rarely outside that awareness. It is only under stress of some great emotion or some tremendous tragedy, severe experience, or shock that the person who has lived in this way for many years may temporarily be outside the kingdom of God. That can and does happen even to those far along on the path, but they have little difficulty remaking their contact. In the early years of our work, however, this is not so. We make the contact and then we seem to lose it for days at a time and find it again only with struggle and strife.

THE FLESH THAT WITHERS

The word *flesh* is used in quite a different sense in the statement, "All flesh is grass." Flesh in that sense means what we behold through the senses, what we see, hear, taste, touch, or smell. As long as we are in a state of consciousness where our demonstration is of persons, things, or conditions, we will not be able to enter the kingdom of God, the realm of the Spirit.

The possession of a billion dollars will not make it possible for a person to inherit the kingdom of God, nor will the belief that flesh has power to give us pleasure or pain. When our faith and confidence are in effects, we will never know the reality of things; we will know only the forms out here. When, however, with study and meditation, our interests begin to transcend people, things, and conditions, we are being led into a higher realm of consciousness; and in that higher realm of consciousness, ultimately, we see Him as He is and we are satisfied with that likeness.

That is also when we begin to understand why it is possible to love one another as neighbors. Once we become aware of one another through this inner mystical vision, we are friends. As a matter of fact, as we see ourselves out here, we are mortal, material, and finite. We are the flesh that withers as the grass; but when we behold ourselves with spiritual vision, in our true identity, we are the children of God. When we awaken from this dream of materiality, we behold persons as they are and are satisfied with that likeness.

As you present yourself to a spiritual teacher with a problem of body, purse, morals, or family relationships, you are of the earth. Your teacher's beholding you that way will never help you solve your problem. But the ability to be still until that little glimpse comes from within enables a spiritual healer to see you as you are, and that reveals the Word made flesh. It reveals the child of God.

REVEALING THE WORD

"The Word was made flesh," the Word—not the words in a book, not the words in a statement, but the Word within. The Word that is God within, that becomes flesh, meaning the Word becomes apparent, visible, audible, and consciously tangible in our experience.

That is why in The Infinite Way it is recommended that beginning students have not less than three periods of meditation every day. These periods may last from one to three or four minutes. It is not good to go beyond that at first because, after a few minutes, meditation is likely to become a mental exercise; then, of course, it loses its power. As one goes on in this study, these periods increase to six, eight, ten, or twelve in a day and from one to five minutes at a time. From then on, the periods themselves may lengthen; and a person may meditate anywhere from two or three to twenty or thirty minutes. But when the meditation becomes a mental practice, it is no longer meditation. The moment you feel a release within, you should stop the meditation. If you cannot get that release, go back to the meditation an hour or two later. Do not sit until the mind begins working because that is not meditation; that is just mental practice. Mental practice is without power.

This does not mean you must give up the practice of pondering, thinking upon, or meditating upon truth. That is quite a different thing from mental practice. When you first sit down to meditate, you may find the mind is loud, noisy, chaotic, and just will not settle down, at least it will not settle down into a degree of quiet wherein you can hear the "still small voice."[8] In that stage, it is wise to take some passage of Scripture or a statement of spiritual wisdom and ponder it, not repeat it as if you expected to gain by repetition, but ponder it for its inner meaning.

This word of truth you are reading is a seed within you that will develop and appear as a state of consciousness.

After that, it will appear outwardly as the health of your body, the adequacy of your purse, a new book, or greater supply. That is the way flesh must be understood. As soon as the flesh is out here, we are done with it. It withers like the grass. Do not put your faith in it. To do so is like putting your faith "in princes."[9]

As you learn to turn within and let the word of truth come into expression, you will find the invisible consciousness or awareness of truth within you becomes externalized as form. It becomes visible flesh, visible form. Then you can do anything you want with the form.

DO NOT GLORY IN THE FORM

As long as you have the consciousness of the Spirit, you can do anything you need to do because it will not be you doing it; it will be the spirit of Truth of which you have become aware. It will take form. But when It does, do not glory in that form. Be very careful you are not satisfied with an abundance of supply, a healthy body, or an everyday happiness. Do not be satisfied with anything in the realm of flesh, in effects or form. I do not mean you should not enjoy things. I mean you should not be satisfied with them.

When you have a satisfactory sense of supply, never rejoice in that as if it were the demonstration. Rejoice in the invisible Spirit that is producing that supply. When a person says to you, "I am feeling better," watch that you do not feel too happy about it because, if you are looking at effects, remember they can change tomorrow. Look behind the individual and be grateful that the conscious awareness of the Spirit has taken place because that is why the person is now well, employed, joyous, or whatever.

Watch that you do not glory in the flesh, in the form of the demonstration, but glory in that other sense of flesh: the Word made flesh. That flesh is the invisible flesh. Over and over metaphysicians lose their whole demonstration of harmony because the moment their income doubles, they think they have made a demonstration. They have, but the demonstration was not the doubled income; the demonstration was the presence of the Spirit that appeared as the doubled income.

The Hebrews who were with the Master thought they had made a demonstration when the loaves and fishes were multiplied. They had not made a demonstration at all. The next day they were hungry again. But the Master had made a demonstration of the consciousness of the presence of God, and so he could multiply loaves and fishes any and every day in the week. He could go out and find gold in the fish's mouth. He was not trying to multiply loaves and fishes; all he was doing was lifting his eyes in the realization that the Spirit of God was his demonstration. To stand in the conscious awareness of the Presence was his demonstration; and when he made that demonstration, the corpse had to jump up, loaves and fishes had to be multiplied, or gold had to be in the fish's mouth, because God is the substance of all form. But if you do not have the presence of God, you cannot have the form.

Do not glory in healing. Never testify to a healing except to illustrate the principle or spiritual idea that brought it about. It is relatively unimportant whether you have health or wealth today. What is important is whether you gain a spiritual conviction that will give you eternal health and eternal wealth. Do not rejoice in any kind of demonstration, but glory and rejoice that you have seen the face of God, that you have borne witness to the presence of the Spirit, which in turn became evident as the healing or as the supply.

KNOWING PERSONS SPIRITUALLY

"Wherefore henceforth know we no man after the flesh: yea, though we have known Christ after the flesh, yet now henceforth know we him no more."[10] Heretofore you have known me in the flesh as a man. Henceforth you are not to know me that way any more, but you are to know me as a spiritual teacher and not judge of the flesh. Heretofore I have known you as human beings and students, but hereafter I must never know you that way again but only as the Christ, as Spirit, as spiritual being, as the offspring of God.

Heretofore you have known your friends, your relatives, your patients, and your students as human beings; some of them good, some of them bad. Henceforth you must know them neither as good nor bad but as spiritual. It is just as wrong to know a person as good as it is to know a person as bad. It is just as wrong to know a person as rich as it is to know a person as poor. You must not know any person after the flesh, whether good flesh or bad. Henceforth you must know a person only as the Christ.

"Therefore if any man be in Christ, he is a new creature: old things are passed away; behold, all things are become new."[11] The moment you give up holding yourself or others in condemnation to being good or bad, sick or well, and know them only after the Spirit, the old things will pass away. Old habits, old forms of the flesh, old fleshly appetites, greed, lust, ambition, desire for health, wealth, and fame—all these things will pass away and all things will become new.

It is on this point that The Infinite Way message stands foursquare. We are not to look on a person as flesh or as a human being. We are not to glory in him as man, good man or bad, but rather now we must know him not after the flesh but after the Spirit. Therefore, if any man be in Christ, if any man be in the consciousness of his Christhood, all the old things will disappear. Even the old associations will drop out of his life. Some of them he may be sad to see go because he enjoyed them, but they will not remain because they will not be a part of his experience any more.

Once we are established in the Christ, our whole family, our whole acquaintanceship, and our whole circle changes. We may even move into a different state or out of the country entirely because all things become new in this higher consciousness in which "we live, and move, and have our being." We find there are no limitations: we are not bound to an apartment or to a house; we are not bound to a family. We have them, but we come and go and feel free.

As consciousness changes and as the substance of Spirit is revealed in consciousness, not necessarily fully revealed but even when it is revealed in part, the Holy Temple, the real body, appears to our awareness. Others may still see it as this form, but we will know that it is not that. This body is the temple of the living God. If we get on a scale, it may still show a certain number of pounds; but we shall have no sense of weight, no sense of solidity, no sense of body.

BEING CLOTHED WITH A NEW CONCEPT OF BODY

"For we know that if our earthly house of this tabernacle were dissolved, we have a building of God, an house not made with hands, eternal in the heavens. For in this we groan, earnestly desiring to be clothed upon with our house which is from heaven. . . . For we that are in this tabernacle do groan, being burdened: not for that we would be unclothed, but clothed upon, that mortality might be swallowed up of life." [12] Our work is not getting rid of, denying, or ignoring the body. Our work is being clothed upon with another consciousness of body, that body that is "not made with hands, eternal in the heavens." This very body is that body. It is eternal in the heavens, immortal. But we cannot see this body. We all will entertain different concepts of every body we see, if we are judging only from appearances based on our experience.

This body, which is invisible, is eternal and immortal and will be with us forever and forever. This body, as I see it, will change from day to day because the higher my concept of God or Spirit, the better looking and better feeling my body becomes. The concept changes, but the body itself is immortal; therefore, we do not get rid of the body even in death. We get rid of our concept of body. Sooner or later we will so evolve in consciousness that our concept of body will change while we are on earth.

A STATE OF AWARENESS

The Word made flesh is not a thought; it is a state of awareness without a conscious thought, and yet at times it appears outwardly as conscious thought. First comes the Word, God, and It becomes flesh. It becomes a state of awareness, but without form. It is not a thought and it is not a thing. But then out of that comes the thought, the spoken word, the written word, the tangible dollar, fish, or loaf of bread. First is the realization of God as Substance. Then the Word, the Substance, becomes flesh. It becomes a state of awareness, a state of consciousness; but it may not necessarily take the form of a thought.

Practitioners will tell you that when that flash of inspiration comes, that release, they do not always have a specific thought with it and yet they have the result as if the thought were there. Sometimes following that may come a specific thought. For example, this morning sitting in my room in meditation, the awareness came; but there was no word or any thought with it. It was just the realization that the lesson today had been given me, and then all of a sudden the word "flesh" came. The state of consciousness achieved in meditation appeared as the word *flesh*, and I knew the lesson was to be on flesh. Simultaneously, out of that word came its double meaning, and out of that meaning came all that is written here.

Never be concerned and never try to have a thought about anything. Never try to know anything about God through the mind because there is no truth you can know consciously that is the truth, so do not be concerned about seeing a vision or hearing words. But neither be disturbed when you see visions or hear words because very often they are a necessary part of your unfoldment.

So it was in California in 1945 that the Voice spoke to me and said the next year would be my year of transition. For a little while, I gave myself very vigorous treatments because I did not feel I was ready to pass on. Then the Voice came again and said, "No, not that type of transition. This is a transition into another state of consciousness."

In July 1946, this change of consciousness began, and the transition lasted two months. At the end of the two months, everything was prepared for this work. The final instruction I was given in this inner experience was this: You will teach, but you will not seek students. You will teach those who are sent to you; and you will teach what is given you to teach.

This work of The Infinite Way was really begun with those two months of actual vision and audible hearing, and yet those experiences have been rare. Usually, the message comes as this lesson has come, with just a feeling, a word, or a passage of Scripture. First comes the inspiration, then the specific thought or idea, and then out of that all the rest. In spiritual consciousness, things unfold that later become flesh in consciousness, invisible flesh; that is, they take form as a state of consciousness and then appear outwardly as words, writings, and recordings.

This kind of flesh—words, writings, and recordings—must wither like the grass. But the flesh, as it is now in my consciousness, will never die; and what you absorb from this chapter in your consciousness will never die. What you put on paper you can probably tear up tomorrow because if you tried to live on it, you would be living on yesterday's manna. What I am giving you now is the seed of truth that came to me from the depth of my withinness as revelation, and it is now being planted in your consciousness. Tomorrow you can close your eyes and find that truth will flow back to you. "And the Word was made flesh, and dwelt among us."

~ 5 ~

OUR REAL IDENTITY

TODAY, with all the conflict, warfare, and turmoil, it appears the world is bent on destroying itself. In this overturning, people of themselves have no strength, intelligence, or love. "For by strength shall no man prevail."[1] This destruction or crucifixion going on throughout the world is really the crucifixion of the belief in personal power, personal will, and the sense of an identity separate and apart from the One. That is all that is being crucified. Anyone holding on to the belief that he has a personal life to save or lose, a personal fortune to protect, or a personal will and dominion may be crucified because those beliefs must be rooted out in order for God's glory to fill the earth and for man to stand forth in the fullness of Christhood.

What can I desire besides Thee? If I had all the earth and Thee, I would have no more than if I just had Thee. But if I had all the earth and had not Thee, then I would have nothing except a void still waiting to be filled.

I realize the uselessness of desiring, wishing, and hoping because in the stillness I know Thou art with me. Thou art the light of my being.

Never can I feel God's presence until I am in the silence. But after I have attained a stillness and silence, I can carry it out into the world for a few hours, when again I must retire for renewal of the assurance. It is not that God is not omnipresent; but in the turmoil of the world and the activity of the human mind, I am apt to develop a sense of separation, a feeling of being apart. So I come back into this silence for a moment to reassure myself and feel that divine Presence.

THE INVISIBILITY OF SPIRITUAL IDENTITY

This life I am experiencing is not my life but God's life: infinite, eternal, and immortal. This body that is my vehicle of expression is God's body. If it were mine, it would be separate and apart from God; and how would I preserve it? But this is not my body; it is the body of God in one of Its infinite forms and expressions. The government is on His shoulder to maintain and sustain this body and its individuality unto eternity. He has promised us He will never leave His universe: He will never leave me or forsake me. That does not mean He will just not leave my soul. It means He will not desert my body either. God does not desert my soul or my body because my soul and body are one. The soul is the essence, and the body is the form.

"Yea, though I walk through the valley of the shadow of death,"[2] You will walk through it with me, and I will find myself with the same individuality and the same body. As my understanding of this grows, however, my physical sense of body will take on an ever better appearance, not because the body changes but because my concept of body changes. My body is always the same: infinite, immortal, useful, vigorous, vital, and eternally youthful. My concept of it may vary. I may accept an aging concept and show it because whatever I accept in my consciousness shows in appearance. But if I accept in my consciousness the truth that this body is the temple of God, formed, maintained, and sustained by God, then I have a concept of eternality much nearer the truth of being. So my body will maintain its matured appearance, its matured strength, and its matured harmony. My body is eternal; only my concept of it changes.

Each year our concept of body improves as we abide in the oneness of all life; and as our concept improves, our appearance improves. God is the principle of all that is: therefore, all that is is eternal. Although we go through the experience the world calls death, we will still be intact, perfect, whole, complete, and spiritual, expressing as a form because there can be no *I* dangling out here in space. *I* is always formed.

When you look at a tree, you actually believe you see a tree. So when the leaves fall off or the branches die, you may think life is not eternal because the flowers, fruits, or branches are dead and you have seen them in their withered state. But you never see a tree. In fact, in all your life, you have never really seen a tree. You have seen the effect or form of a tree, but the tree itself is as invisible as you and I are.

If I want to see you, it is only in the very height of my illumined moments that I can contact the reality of the you that is you, what you know when you say, "I." If you were to close your eyes right now and say, "I, Mary," "I, George," or whatever your name is, you would know at once I could not see you because that

Mary or that George is nowhere visible. The body is not you: the head is yours; the neck is yours; the arms are yours; all of the body down to the feet is yours; but it is never you.

Who knows you? Who knows me? Who has ever seen you or me? Each one of you has a concept of me, and there are as many different concepts of me as there are persons entertaining those concepts. I would recognize none of them as being Joel because I know myself within, and you do not. You merely have formed an opinion about me, a concept: sometimes good, sometimes bad, but never correct because whatever I am, I am. That is my real selfhood, which I do not show to anybody. I do not let anyone know what I am like in my worst moments, but my good moments I hide, too. My Self is hidden inside all alone, safe in God. So I show forth only certain qualities, and on those you form a concept or opinion.

I, too, form concepts and opinions of you. Sometimes I erroneously state I do not think this or that student will ever arrive anywhere spiritually, and then he confounds me by being one of the best. Furthermore, the Judases, the Peters, and the doubting Thomases show us how wrong our concepts can be when we vest them with all the glories of pure spirituality and then they fail to live up to that confidence and trust.

Many of you in metaphysics have been taught every person is a spiritual idea, the child of God, and that cats, dogs, and flowers are spiritual ideas. That is not true and never was. A spiritual idea is perfect and eternal in the heavens. A spiritual idea never changes, never lacks, never has a sense of separation from God, never grows old, and never dies. It can never be seen with the eyes, never. Just as you cannot see me because that "me" is a spiritual idea, so you cannot see a cat, a dog, a flower, or a tree. You can see only the form. The spiritual idea is the entity itself, which is the spiritual identity; but what you behold is your concept of that spiritual identity.

You cannot see my hand. You do not even know what a hand is. Look at your hand and then understand that you are not seeing it. You are seeing your concept of it appearing as form. The hand itself is a permanent spiritual idea and never changes, never ages, or never dies. It is an instrument for your use, provided for you in the beginning; and it will be with you eternally.

The purpose of The Infinite Way teaching is to lead you to that state of consciousness in which, when you see a discordant person, thing, or condition, you do not attempt to change it. Do not try to manipulate anything in the external. Realize you are not beholding anything but a concept that, in and of itself, has no power, presence, or reality. The reality of what you are witnessing is eternal in the heavens, perfect. As you look at a harmonious body, a youthful body, or a physically perfect body, remember you are not seeing a spiritual idea. You are seeing your *concept* of a spiritual idea. When you understand that, you will begin to heal, and the healings will come quickly.

MAINTAINING THE SPIRITUAL HEIGHTS OF CONSCIOUSNESS

Healing is an activity of individual consciousness. It does not take place because of any mysterious God. As far as God is concerned, God is; and God is eternally omnipresent as individual you and me. To God, there can be no such thing as a healing.

Some persons engaged in spiritual work have a beautiful healing consciousness; others have not attained that consciousness; and still others are on the way toward attaining it. No person engaged in healing work lives at the standpoint of full spiritual consciousness at every given moment or is at all times at the peak of spiritual awareness. When he is, healings are beautiful and quick; but when he is not, a struggle takes place.

Very often practitioners or teachers are not at the highest level because patients and students will not permit them to take the necessary forty days to go up to the mountains and abide there. They will not give them weekends or whatever time is required, and gradually they pull them down to their own level. Then comes the struggle, and spiritual healers have to get away for long periods of time.

There is no such thing as attaining spiritual consciousness and maintaining it forever without a continuity of effort. No one can jump into heaven in this life and remain there. The mesmerism of the human world is such that a person is in a continuous state of fluctuation: up today, and down tomorrow, or up for a week and down for a day. Those practitioners who know how to withdraw from the world six hours a day to where they cannot even hear the telephone ring very often are able to maintain the highest state of consciousness. Practitioners or teachers who most nearly keep their thought filled with God's will as the only will and God's law as the only law keep their consciousness on such a high level that every contact with them results in upliftment in some degree.

There is nothing mysterious about healing; and it has nothing to do with God because, in the realm of God, perfection is. It is a question of your and my ability to maintain ourselves on the spiritual heights. One way is to find the particular inspirational literature that helps keep consciousness on that level. It makes no difference whether it is in the form of books of inspirational prose, poetry, or Scripture. It must be something that maintains us, not on an emotional level but on a spiritual level of a high degree.

A spiritual level of a high degree has nothing to do with emotion. It has nothing to do with your feeling that you are walking on a cloud. Spiritual consciousness is a state of consciousness that fears neither persons nor conditions. It looks out on this world and says, "I love you whether you are good or bad, in pain or without pain." It understands that God is the center of power, life, love and activity. It does not look to "man, whose breath is in his nostrils."[3] It does not put its faith in "princes,"[4] dollar bills, medicine bottles, climate, or weather. Its whole faith is in the kingdom of God established within.

ONENESS, AN ETERNAL RELATIONSHIP

We are tempted daily to believe in a separation from God. One person may have some little or great sin come into his life and be certain that is enough to separate him from God. Another person feels she has made a mistake of some kind, some act of omission or commission, that is going to separate her. Another person becomes the victim of a serious disease and thinks that is a sign of separation from God. Still another person goes through a period of lack or limitation and accepts that as evidence that she is separate and apart from God, and in that acceptance lies the continuation of her trouble. Oneness with the Father is an eternal relationship. All you can entertain is a *sense* of separation from God, never a separation from God. The *sense* of separation from God can be overcome by knowing the truth:

I am never separated from God. All the sins I have ever committed or ever may commit will never separate me from the love of God. Not all the lack or limitation will convince me I have become separated from the Father or we are apart from one another. And not all the diseases, even unto death, will ever make me believe God has deserted me. In spite of the fact that at this moment I am entertaining a sense of separation from God, God is; and I abide in God's isness.

Break that sense of separation not by trying to make a demonstration in space or in time but by withdrawing into that inner sanctuary, becoming very still, and beginning again with everything you have learned to reassure yourself of the permanent nature of your being and true identity.

"Before Abraham was, I am." [5] *I will live unto eternity. I will never be forsaken or forgotten. I will never be without the life of God and the love of God, the Spirit of God and the Soul of God. If for any reason, I have soiled or am soiling that temple of God, there is lots of soap and water. I will scrub it clean with the realization that the true nature of my being is God.*

"For the good that I would I do not: but the evil which I would not, that I do."[6] Part of our human nature is expressed in that statement of Paul's, but "forgetting those things which are behind,"[7] looking up into the future, going forward, now in this moment of awareness, we begin to climb anew. If we can be generous enough to forgive our neighbor "seventy times seven,"[8] we certainly can be that generous with ourselves and forgive ourselves, knowing in the depths of our being we are pure and our motives are pure. In the depths of our being, we are clean, and whatever uncleanness there is about us represents only that mesmerism of the human world that we have not completely overcome and that even the Master did not overcome until near the end of his great ministry when he said, "I have overcome the world."[9]

When we are resurrected, that is, when we have "died daily" to such a degree that we have come into the conscious realization of our true being, then we, too, will be able to say, "I have overcome the world." We have overcome the world when we no longer hate, fear, love, worship, or trust anyone or anything in the world and yet love because we see the Spirit of God at the center of all being. Then we can look at every person in the flesh and recognize we are not seeing him because he is invisible.

It was difficult for anyone to see Jesus in his true being. Only Peter recognized him as the Christ. So you, too, will keep looking at a person and saying, "There is James, John, or Elizabeth," until one day you will look through that appearance and say, "No, there is the Christ." Every practitioner or teacher looks at the human appearance and rejects it: "No, no, no, you are not James, John, or Elizabeth. You are the Christ. I do not see that with my eyes, I see it with my inner eye. I recognize you; I salute the Christ of God."

The world's concept of you is visible, but you your-self are shining out from behind your eyes. That *you* is the invisible Christ or child of God; and now, just as you are looking out through adult eyes, remember there was a time when you were looking out through an infant's eyes and another time when you were looking out through a child's eyes. But always it was you looking out through those eyes, the invisible you.

I am hid with Christ in God. I am invisible to the world. That is why the weapons of the world cannot touch me because I am not in the world. I am invisible.

As you come to that point, your consciousness becomes spiritually enriched with the grace of God beyond anything you have brought about with your right thinking or right knowing, your right reading or right meditating. In other words, you carry yourself to a certain degree of unfoldment by knowing the correct truth about God, man, and the universe. You enrich your consciousness by every spiritual message you read, study, ponder, and meditate upon. But over and above that is the added measure given to you by the grace of God, which brings about the real spiritualization of your being. What you do is only a preparation for what you receive.

PRAYER, A STATE OF RECEPTIVITY

Answered prayer is the result of a divine Impulse felt or sensed within. It has nothing to do with anything you do but is something of which you become aware. Your thoughts or statements are but preparations for receiv-ing prayer and its answer. All this truth being stated here is not prayer. It is a preparation of consciousness to receive the word of God, and it is the word of God that is prayer. It is the word of God that is powerful; it is the word of God that heals—not your word, not mine, not your thoughts, and not mine. "For my thoughts are not your thoughts."[10]

What I declare in silence is not prayer. It is a preparation for prayer and meditation. Then, when I am through with all that, even though they have been beautiful thoughts or statements, I become quiet; and God prays in me, that is, God utters Its word in me. What I become aware of is the word of God; and when I look out here, I see what I received inwardly opened the Red Sea outwardly.

The Word I received in silence, secrecy, and sacredness went ahead of me to heal or enlighten the patient or student. I did not send out a good thought to him. I did not instruct him or heal him. Through the silence and a calm reassurance, I opened my consciousness to a receptivity to the word of God, the divine Impulse. When It came and I felt It, I knew It was out here making deserts blossom, making sick bodies well, and making unemployed people employed. It was doing it. I was merely a state of receptivity, receiving the word of God in my consciousness and then letting It flow.

Never have a prayer, communion, or meditation period in which you do all the talking or thinking and then think you have accomplished anything. Do not place yourself in the position of expecting God to listen to your words or thoughts most of the time. The right attitude is for you to be waiting for God to speak to you.

We use words and thoughts in prayer and meditation only to lift us up until we get high enough to apprehend the Word. It will not be understood through the human mind. It will not come to us through the turmoil of our thinking, unless, in rare cases, there is some tremendous impact and through that shock something breaks through. But God is heard in the quietness and peacefulness of the silence, and it is only in quietness and peacefulness that we become attuned to God. God is omnipresence, God is here, and God is now. God is in the midst of any and every turmoil, but we do not become aware of that Presence except in the quietness of our soul and the stillness of our mind.

When the human mind is still, there is completeness, fulfillment, and a realization of spiritual identity. It is only in the human mind that the turmoil of life goes on. Once you rise above that, there is no turmoil; there are no problems; and there is nothing out of which problems could arise because everything that concerns your welfare is supplied from the infinite Source. The moment you are completely released from human concern, your good begins to flow and you find it always there just before you need it.

As long as the human mind is active, we will feel lack and limitation, and we will desire to have that emptiness filled. Then we will go out and struggle to fill it; whereas after we have come to a place in our meditation where we can sit down and slide right into the rhythm of the universe, desire disappears. There is no desire: there is just being in tune with the rhythm of perfect harmony.

When I am thus centered, life flows with no conscious effort. I am not making the stars come out or the moon rise or the sun set. I am not trying to make flowers grow. I am just resting from labor. I am resting from the tiredness of thought, and I am perfectly content to let God run the universe.

No Time or Space in God

The very nature of God makes infinity an assured truth. That which God creates is never extinguished. If God has given us our individuality, if God has given us our being and our body, then we must have these eternally because the work of God is forever. In God, there is no such thing as time and space. God is, and that is all we know. God does not work in time and space; God works in the infinite nowness. There is no time in God any more than there is time in your life. Time is just something with which you measure outer events, but you do not live in time; you live in the infinite nature of your being.

Some of you may remember the story of the man in a rowboat on a stream. At the place and time he started his trip, it was here and now; but the place to which he was going was over there and later. In other words, it was in the future and it was off in space; but when he got there, he found it was here and now. The place that had been here and now was there and then, and the place to which he was going was there later. Everything was turned around; but when he arrived at the last place, everything behind him was there and then and all his hereness and nowness had gone except that he carried it with him to where he was. As far as he was concerned, it was still here and now. Later he had an opportunity to go up in a balloon. When he did, he found these places are all here and all now. He could see them and feel them and be aware of them from the heights as the very hereness and nowness. There was neither time nor space in those three.

As you close your eyes, you are less aware of time and space; but as you meditate and finally achieve the

center of your being, all sense of time, space, and body
disappears: weight, concern, the past, and the future. All
those things disappear and you find yourself just living.
There is no sense of the past, no sense of the future.
There is no sense of a desire, because in that deep
mystical consciousness of hereness and nowness there
is only fulfillment.

ESTABLISHING THE REIGN OF DIVINE GOVERNMENT INDIVIDUALLY

God made me, so it is God's responsibility to maintain and sustain me, to feed, house, and clothe me. If I
am to receive justice, recognition, reward, or compensa-
tion, it is God's responsibility.

*The government of my life is on Thy shoulders. I abide in
Thee; and I know that Thou abidest in me, for we are one.
Thou abidest in my fellow man, and so I and my fellow man
are one. Thou abidest in the animals, vegetables, and minerals
as Thou abidest in me; so I am one with them. We are not
enemies. We are friends; we are brothers in Christ.*

*I am in Thee, and Thou in me, I in You, and You in me,
an infinite Oneness of being, the one love permeating all
creation, the one life permeating all being, the one substance
forming all creation, the one law holding us all in our relationship to it and to each other.*

*The government is upon Thy shoulders to maintain me in
Thy image and likeness and forever to maintain my relationship with the human, animal, mineral, and vegetable species.
If I were at the bottom of the sea, Thou wouldst still be in me.
As I fly high in the heavens, Thou art with me. There is the
same sustaining influence under the seas, on the earth, or in
the air.*

Thy grace is not removed from me, though I ride beneath the waves, on the waves, on the surface of the land, or in the air. Thy grace is the same. Safety is in Thee, so I have no concern for vehicles because safety is not in vehicles. I am always consciously aware that my concern is only that I am one with Thee. In that awareness, I know Thou wilt never leave me or forsake me; we are one. "For thine is the kingdom, and the power, and the glory."[11]

There is no power apart from Thee. There is no realm or kingdom apart from Thine. Whether we behold it as land or sea or air, it is all Thy kingdom. Thine is the kingdom: the kingdom of earth, the kingdom of water, the kingdom of the air. Thine is the kingdom.

Thy law governs. Thy light, wisdom, and illumination are forever shining. Thine is the kingdom. It is as much Thy kingdom in Russia as it is in the United States because neither Russia nor the United States is truly Thy kingdom, but our concept of Thy kingdom. But Thy kingdom is established there. It makes no difference if we call it Vietnam, Indonesia, the United Kingdom, or the Union of South Africa. The truth of being is that these are Thy kingdom. Thy presence is as much on earth as it is in heaven. "Thine is the kingdom, and the power, and the glory."

THE BIRTHLESS, DEATHLESS CHRIST

Relax and rest in the assurance that God is in the midst of you. The Father that dwells in you never leaves you. "I stand at the door, and knock."[12] This is the Christ, the son of God, speaking to you: "I stand at the door, and knock." Forever and forever, the Christ keeps knocking at your door, when you are sinning, when you are dying, and even when you are dead. Christ never stops knocking at the door until in this lifetime or some future lifetime you open that door.

The door is not outside of you, and the Christ is not outside of you knocking to get in. The Christ is inside you, and the door is inside. It is the door of your consciousness, and the Christ is trying to be released into your experience by your recognizing and admitting It. The way you admit the Christ is not to believe the Christ lived two thousand years ago and died and was resurrected and will come again. If you believe that, you will never open the door for the Christ.

The Christ was never born and will never die. The Christ was with you "before Abraham" and will be with you unto the end of the world. There was no birth of the Christ, and there will be no second birth. The Christ is within you and is your real identity; the Christ stands at the door of your consciousness and knocks.

"Before Abraham was," the Christ was in me. The Christ will be with me unto the end of the world, and now I accept the Christ in the midst of me and acknowledge that the Christ is the word of God, which becomes flesh in my life. I acknowledge the Christ in the midst of me.

Now I open the door of my consciousness to admit the Christ that It may take over, be my life, be my savior, be the divine Presence in me. Henceforth, I look to Thee, the Christ within me, rather than to "man, whose breath is in his nostrils" or rather than to powers out here.

The Christ lives in me eternally. The Christ is my life. The Christ is my meat, my wine, and my water. The Christ is the resurrection of my body, of my business, of my home. The Christ is the resurrection unto all my affairs.

The Christ is not a man. The Christ is the Spirit of God in man, the Spirit that God placed in me "before Abraham was."

In the beginning, God placed His Spirit, His son, His life within me; and this enables me to say, "I have meat to eat that ye know not of." [13] *What is this meat I have? The Christ within, the all-power, the only power. I shall not fear anything or anybody in the external realm.*

When you have accepted the Christ in the midst of you, your whole world begins to change because you are not in the world alone. Now you have the divine Presence, the divine Power, the infinite All; and It goes before you to "make the crooked places straight."[14] It dissolves erroneous appearances "not by might, nor by power,"[15] but by the gentle Spirit of the Christ. "Stand still, and see the salvation of the Lord"[16] that is within you, the Power, the Presence, the divine Grace that is within you. Open the door of your consciousness and recognize that in the beginning God planted His son in you, His very Spirit. God breathed His own life into you as your life. "I live; yet not I, but Christ liveth in me."

Every time you hear the word of God in your ear, the Word will become new flesh. Every time you relax in the Spirit of God, you will find some part of your body being renewed, rebuilt, reborn, and resurrected because the Word becomes flesh.

~ 6 ~

THE WORD AND WORDS

MANY persons believe what is written in Scripture and in metaphysical books is Truth, the Word. But it really is not that at all. It is merely a collection of statements about Truth. It is never Truth Itself. Truth is your consciousness of Truth; it is your awareness of Truth. That is the only Truth there is, and that is the Word.

The Word is never an effect; it is cause. When the word of God comes to you, not from outside but from within yourself, then if you have a Red Sea to cross, It will open it. If you are in the desert, the desert will blossom; if you need rain, rain will fall; if you need sun, the sun will shine; if you need food, food will appear; if you need money, money will appear. These things will come about because the word of God is the substance of life, and out of this Word comes the flesh or form: your body, your business, your home, your profession, your ability, your customers, your clients, or your supply.

Even though you read these words, they are not yet power insofar as you are concerned. Even if they sound reasonable to you and you can accept the message intellectually, it still is not power with you. It becomes power only when you have buried it in your consciousness and pondered it until from a depth within you the answer and an acceptance of it, which might be called a conviction or realization, comes. The statements in a book—the words, sentences, and paragraphs—represent the truth about the Truth, leading you back to the depths of your own withinness, where you make room for the Word to come forth.

KNOWING THE TRUTH IN CONTEMPLATIVE MEDITATION

If you were about to give a treatment or have a contemplative meditation, you would bring to conscious remembrance every thought and idea you could about God and spiritual creation—not about man, not about a patient, not about the disease, the sin, or the lack. There is no truth you can know about man except that of himself he is nothing. But you can know the truth about God, and it is this that constitutes your treatment or meditation. So you might sit quietly and remind yourself:

God is; and because God is one, God is infinite, and God is all there is. God is present where I am.

God is the only law because God is the lawgiver. Because God is the only law, there is no law of disease, no law of lack, no law of limitation. God is law, the law of abundance. God is omnipotent power, all-powerful law; so there is no law opposing God's law, and God Is the law unto my individual being.

God is love, so there is no power opposing God's love.

God is life, therefore, there is no disease in life and there is no death in life.

God is consciousness, infinite, immortal, divine Consciousness; so there is no unconsciousness.

God is infinite intelligence; and therefore, there is no such thing as insanity, lack of intelligence, or any mortal belief of retardation. There is no truth to them; there is no power in them because God is the only power.

Regardless of any sin, disease, death, lack, or limitation I am beholding, there is no power in it. There is no power in the appearance of sin, disease, death, lack, or limitation. So if it wants to keep on being, let it go ahead and be; but there is no power in it. There is no power aside from God.

That is the truth about the Truth; but when you have declared all the truth about God and God's creation that you know, you sit back in a listening, attentive attitude and now the Word—the W-O-R-D—will come to you. You may hear It within you as if you were hearing a voice; you may see a flash of light; or you may just get a feeling, a deep breath, and then a release, as if a weight had dropped off your shoulder. We call that hearing the Word even though you have heard no audible word.

When you use the language of religion and Scripture, you may indulge somewhat in poetic license. When you say you hear the "still small voice,"[1] it does not necessarily mean you hear anything. Some times it just means you take a deep breath, a smile comes to your face, and you wonder what you could have been troubled about. All appearances may be the same, but now you are released and set free of them. It is as if you looked at a bowl of flowers, saw them as snakes, and for a minute became frightened. Then when you looked again and realized they were flowers, you were relieved—no more fear. The same thing was there that caused you to fear before, but now it does not cause fear because you have been released from the false concept of it.

BELIEF VERSUS EXPERIENCE

If you think of a disease as being something to fear, as dangerous and harmful, or if you think of lack as something you must get rid of, naturally you are going to fear it. As long as you fear anything, you are enslaved by it. But in a period of illumination, you say to yourself, "Why should I fear disease? God is the only power, so what power can disease have? Why should I fear lack? What possible difference does it make whether I have a lot of money in my pocket or a little? God still is functioning. That's all I have to care about. If there is a God, I am happy and safe. If there isn't, I have something to be fearful about. But just fearing the lack of money or the lack of home is nonsense as long as there is God."

Begin to fear if you discover there is no God because then you are in trouble. But as long as you can have the assurance there is God, do not fear a condition, do not fear a person, do not fear a bomb. The decision is yours. Do you believe there is a God? I do not mean believe as most persons are taught to believe, but do you believe in God? "Oh yes," you may reply. "I believe in God." "What do you believe about God?" "I don't know." Such a person does not really believe in God; inwardly, he questions the existence of God. No one should have that kind of a belief about God. Real belief in God comes when a person experiences God. He experiences God when he experiences the Word, which means the consciousness or feeling of the Presence. He begins with statements of truth; but the moment he feels the Word, his Red Sea begins to open, his desert begins to blossom, his supply begins to flow, and his health begins to be restored.

KNOWING THE TRUTH ABOUT WHAT IS

There is no truth to know about man, so do not waste time knowing the truth about Jones, Brown, or Smith. "If I bear witness of myself, my witness is not true."[2] So if you speak of Jones, Brown, Smith, or yourself, you are speaking a lie. Do not know the truth about man, and do not try to know the truth about sin, disease, and death. There is none; they are illusions.

If you were on the desert and you saw the mirage of water ahead of you, would you try to know the truth about that water? You cannot do that because there is no truth to know about the water. The water is an illusion. You would have to know the truth about the desert, and the desert is made up of many things—sun, sand, and air. That is the truth. What happens to the mirage? You see right through it. You may still see the image of water there, but now it has no power over you. You do not fear it; you do not try to go around it; and you do not call the fire department to pump it away. You go right through it because you are not going through water; you are going through a mirage. What you understand as nothingness has no power to limit you.

Suppose you declare that disease has no power and no law, and then you look to see if the disease is still there. That is no different from declaring there is no water on the desert because it is a mirage and still accepting the mirage as real and as a hindrance. As long as you thought the water you saw on the desert was water, you would be in bondage to it. You could not go through it. You would be looking for a way around it or a way to get rid of it; but the minute you knew the water was a mirage and it had no power, you would start your car and go right through it. It has no power to bind you once you know that what you called water was not water but a mirage.

DEALING WITH WHAT APPEARS AS BELIEF

As long as you think of disease, knowing its ultimate is pain, death, or dissolution, you cannot help fearing it, hating it, and wanting to get rid of it. But the minute you can say, "Oh, you are not disease: you are a mirage; you are an illusion; you are a lie about God," it does not matter if you still see it. It has lost its power over you when you can see there is no God-power in it, no power of any nature in it. Because it has lost its power over you, even though the appearance may still continue for a day, a week, or a month, be assured it will gradually fade out of your consciousness once you are released from your hatred of it, fear of it, or desire to get rid of it.

That is a very deep point because in this state of consciousness, you are to make no effort to get rid of sin, disease, or death, which you could not do any more than the alcoholic can get free of his snakes. If he is seeing snakes in his alcoholic dream, they are going to stay with him as long as he is in bondage to the alcohol. The effect of alcohol may be such that he believes he sees snakes; and as long as he is suffering from the effects of an excessive indulgence in alcohol, he will continue to see snakes.

Sin, disease, and death represent a belief of a self-hood apart from God, a power and a presence apart from God. So as long as you have the belief of a self-hood, a presence, and a power apart from God, the substance of that belief will be present in the form of disease, lack, limitation, or sin. There is no use trying to get rid of it. The thing to do is to try to change your idea about it or attain the consciousness or awareness of truth.

LISTENING FOR THE WORD

In spiritual teaching, words refer to anything and everything you know about God, God's law, God's presence, God's power, God's being, God's man, God's universe, and God's kingdom. That is the word about God or Truth; but when you become quiet and feel a release, that is *the* Word, that is the consciousness or awareness of God's presence. That is God's presence announcing Itself within you. The word of God is power, great power, infinite power, the only power: quick and sharp.

If the words you and I declare were the word of God, they also would be quick and sharp and powerful. We would only have to think or voice words, and all error would disappear. But our words—what we read, state, or think—are not the word of God. The words we know, think, read, state, or declare about God and God's universe constitute the truth about the Truth, the word about the Truth. Then, after knowing the truth, we can meditate: "Father, I have lifted myself into Your consciousness. Reveal Yourself; declare Yourself."

Take a listening attitude. You may have to train yourself for a week, a month, or a year before you really get to the point where you can settle down into an atmosphere of receptivity and wait until that beautiful release comes from within you. If you seek it and want

it, you can have it. You have the whole kingdom of God
in your grasp; but because of centuries of humanhood,
you have lost the ability to contact it. If you want the
kingdom of God enough, you will learn to sit down two
or three times a day, remind yourself of every truth you
can remember about God and God's kingdom and
God's universe and God's creation, and then rest back:

*Now, Father, You speak. I am listening for Your voice. I
am receptive to Your presence. I have only one desire—nothing
out here. I am not interested in achieving place, position,
wealth, fame, fortune, or happiness—not even peace, not even
security. I have only one desire in life: to know You. That is
my only desire. I surrender this whole world to You, Father;
I will give back to You everybody and everything in it. Just let
me have You. Right now I ask no blessings for myself or for
anybody else. Only let me know You.*

MATERIAL MAN, A GETTER; SPIRITUAL MAN, A GIVER

Mortal, material man is a go-getter, always "on the
make," out to get something, but never arriving, never
satisfied. Even when he has succeeded in getting his
millions—the presidency, name, or fame—always there is
one step more to go; and he never achieves peace,
harmony, home, satisfaction, or joy.

Spiritual man is the opposite of that. Spiritual man
never needs anything. Spiritual man has all that the
Father has and is, therefore, always seeking ways to let
it flow. In other words, it is always pouring through
him. Whatever he has is never his personal possession.

Man, once he comes into the awareness of his true
being, is not a getter or a taker. To outward appearances, he is a giver; yet he is not really a giver. He is

like the pane of glass through which the sun shines. He is only an instrument, an outlet, because he never gives anything of his own. He has nothing to give any more than I have these words of truth to give. They are not mine; they are just coming through me. If I ever tried to store them up, I would forget them. So the best thing for me to do is to let them flow while they are flowing, loose them, and let them go. This is true of everything in life. It is true of cooperation and friendliness, of sharing, whether of money or ideas. On every plane of life, spiritual man is never seeking.

The minute there is a thought in your mind of getting or receiving, even from God, you are back in mortality again. It is only when you are realizing "I have" and letting it loose that you are in spiritual awareness. You are in spiritual consciousness as long as you are in the consciousness that good is flowing through you to the world. The moment the thought of getting or receiving comes in, even being worthy of or deserving of, then you are off the spiritual beam.

TRUTH KNOWN WITH THE MIND

Actually, there is no truth you know that is really the Truth. Real Truth is something not known with the mind: It is something that imparts Itself to the soul. The truth we know with the mind is only our preparation for receiving the Word Itself in the soul.

Affirmations and denials of truth are not used in The Infinite Way. Passages of Scripture or spiritual literature are used for inspiration. But there is a difference between repeating the quotation, "For he performeth the thing that is appointed for me,"[3] some hundred times,

more or less, and taking the statement into meditation
and pondering it until it is revealed who the "he" is that
is referred to and what is "appointed" for you. Learn to
turn within to let the Father give you the passage that is
to be your manna for the day. Talking about God,
reading about God, or going to classes to learn about
God will not be your salvation. But doing these things
will lead to your salvation if you will be steadfast. Your
salvation will come only when you realize and recognize the Spirit of God in your experience, when you
have an actual God-experience.

You may have many healings. You may witness
much in the way of supply and happiness coming to you
through the illumined consciousness of a practitioner or
teacher; but that does not make for permanent harmony. That does not come until such time as you abide
in the word of Truth and let that Word abide in you,
until the experience of God is yours.

As you listen to the "still small voice" in your inner
being, one of these days you will hear it say: "Thou art
my son; thou art my beloved son; thou art the Christ of
God; in thee I am well pleased." But it is "the mouth of
the Lord" that will say that to you, not a practitioner, a
teacher, a diploma, or a title. It will be "the mouth of
the Lord" Itself that will utter these words in your
consciousness, and then you will know that the Spirit of
the Lord God is upon you. "And they shall call them,
The holy people, The redeemed of the Lord: and thou
shalt be called, Sought out, A city not forsaken."[4]

That is what you will be called in that moment when
you realize the Spirit of the Lord God is upon you. That
is why I say you should not spend your time doing
mental work or spend all your time reading. Give

plenty of time to contemplation and meditation. Contemplate and meditate upon God and the things of God until the very Spirit of God Itself proclaims Its presence within your consciousness.

THE LISTENING PERIOD IN TREATMENT

When you are called upon for help, even though at first you may use treatment, be sure your treatment consists of the word God and then the reminder to yourself of all you know and understand about God and God's kingdom. When that period has come to an end, do not think you are finished. The sense of being finished comes only when the second half has been completed and you are able to sit in the silence and listen until the Spirit of God is upon you and you know that It is. You feel It; you have the response within you.

Over and over, I have stressed there is no truth you know with your mind that is really true. There is no truth you ever declare or read in a book that is really true. These are only statements or thoughts about the Truth: words, not *the* Word. There is no external thing that can be called God. Because God is truth, there is no external thing that can be called Truth.

Perhaps this is the most important point in all healing practice: do not put too much faith in what you hear or what you read. Put your real faith and confidence in your ability to sit quietly and listen. Be still. It requires no thoughts and no words to induce the Spirit of God to fall upon you. It requires stillness, quietness, and confidence. Sit in quietness and let "My peace"[5] come to you. It is a peace beyond all knowledge, a peace no one can describe and no one can give to you. That peace is from God; and even though it may appear to come to you through some person, it is from God.

Your relationship to God is oneness, divine sonship. Regardless of anything or anybody else in the world, that is your relationship. You can always realize that Oneness by going to a quiet place in your home, a public library, or a church where no service is in progress—any place you can be still, quiet, and at peace—and be in an atmosphere of God. Wherever you are, in that state of quietness, the grace of God is available to you because of your divine sonship, because of your oneness with the Father, and not because you deserve it as a human being. There are no human beings in the world who can ever be good enough to deserve the grace of God.

Even in the deepest of sins, the grace of God can come to you. Having that Grace, the sins will disappear, the disease will drop away—not always instantly because sometimes the outward evidence of the grace of God comes slowly. Therefore, I urge you to be patient with yourself and thereby learn to be patient with others who find themselves in varying forms of disease, sin, lack, or limitation. Never be impatient with your progress or with anyone else's.

The grace of God comes slowly to most of us, not because of God but because of the density of our humanhood. If all our sins do not disappear in a second, we do not judge, criticize, or condemn. If our outer lives do not immediately attest to the fullness of this message, we do not think there is something wrong with the message. Each of us in this work is trying to live up to his or her highest demonstrated state of Christ-consciousness, and the fact that we are continuing in this

work shows we are struggling to attain even higher
realms of spiritual consciousness, deeper visions of the
Christ. So be very gentle and generous in your opinions
of what degree of attainment you and others have
already achieved.

THE SPIRIT OF THE LORD

When you have loved ones—family, friends, patients,
or students—who appeal to you for help, do not permit
yourself to be upset about their problems. Compel
yourself to sit in the silence and receive the Spirit of
God within you. As you experience that Spirit of the
Lord, your friend, your relative, your patient, or your
student will be lifted into a higher consciousness and
will also experience harmony, grace, and peace.

It is not a concern for the world that will enable you
to help the world. It is not being a do-gooder or having
a zeal to proselytize that will bring healing or comfort or
supply. One thing alone will enable you to be a light to
this world and that is the ability to sit in quietness and
in peace and feel the Spirit of the Lord God upon you.
Then that Spirit of the Lord you feel within you will be
the saving and healing Grace to all those within range
of your consciousness.

The moment the Spirit of the Lord God is upon you,
every word you speak or write to your relatives, friends,
patients, or students goes out all over the world. You do
not know the limit of your capacity once you have felt
the Spirit of the Lord within your consciousness. Every
letter you write that carries a message of truth is an
expansion of your conscious awareness of the Spirit of
the Lord God within you reaching out to the heart, soul,

consciousness, and body of those to whom you write. That Spirit in you is an expansion of spiritual consciousness encircling the globe.

THE WORD, NOT WORDS, BRINGS FORTH SPIRITUAL FRUITAGE

Truth is infinite, and all the truth is in your consciousness this minute. Therefore, you do not have to learn any truth. The only reason you are studying this book is to bring that truth forth from within into conscious realization. Because God is your consciousness, your consciousness is already full and complete; it has in it now all the truth you will ever need until the end of time. Even the Bible cannot add to that. You have only to turn to the Father within to have whatever truth you need at this moment revealed to you. It will be the Word, not words.

If you have had the experience of being the instrument through which a hundred cases of rheumatism were healed, you might think that for the hundred and first case it would be necessary simply to remember the truth used in dealing with the previous hundred cases. But that would be of no help. With each problem, it is necessary to turn within to the Father, to your own divine Consciousness, for the truth of that moment. This clearly reveals why it is impossible to develop a formula for healing because healing is not the fruitage of words, but comes when *the* Word is heard.

Any truth out in the world in any form is an effect, not a cause. The only truth that is a cause is the truth that unfolds from within your own being. But when the word of God comes through, it "is quick, and powerful, and sharper than any two edged sword, piercing even to the dividing asunder of soul and spirit, and of the joints and marrow, and is a discerner of the thoughts and intents of the heart."[6]

When we are faced with a problem, we sit in the silence. In order to be able to do that, we begin with a conscious realization of God and whatever statements we can remember about God; but that is not for the purpose of healing anybody of anything. It is for the purpose of getting ourselves quiet and receptive in an attitude of assurance. Then we sit back and say, "Father, it is Your turn," and remain in peace and quiet until something comes. The word of God may come as a statement or just as a feeling of release. If the healing is not brought out, it may be necessary to go through this process a second time or two hundred times. This clearly is not a dependence on words, no matter how true and authoritative they may be. It is complete reliance on the Word.

Statements are taken into contemplative meditation, pondered, and reflected upon so their inner meaning is revealed. When you receive their inner meaning, you are being spiritually fed. Meditation is not a ritual, not cut and dried. Sometimes it may be completed in almost the blink of an eye, and at other times it may be necessary to sit up all night or to continue with periodic meditations for many weeks. Healing does not come until you have been lifted out of the belief that the problem has power. It may take many meditations to arrive at that consciousness, which is the freedom. Statements of truth do not bring freedom. Freedom is a state of consciousness within, and it brings the release for you or for anyone turning to you.

The object of our work is the unfoldment of mystical consciousness to that point where we can spiritually apprehend the truth about ourselves and each other. That comes only when the Spirit of the Lord God is upon us and "the mouth of the Lord" gives us our new name, which is Son, Son of Righteousness, the Christ. It is out of the Lord's mouth that we receive the new name Christ, Beloved, the beloved one of Israel, *My* son. We hear that in our ear in quietness and stillness, and that is the Spirit of the Lord God that falls upon us.

PART III.

ATTAINING
CONSCIOUS DOMINION

~ 7 ~

CONCEPTS OR IS?

IF I were to ask you what you think about the Bible, your opinion would most likely be different from the opinion of everyone else reading this book. There seems to be very little agreement on the subject of the Bible. But no matter what you or anyone else believes about it, it is what it is; and what it is no one really knows. If you had been asked a year ago about it and then again today and again a year from now, probably none of the three answers would agree because your concept of the Bible changes with the unfoldment of your consciousness.

So, too, whatever you may be thinking about a person is wrong. I do not care what you are thinking. Whatever it is, it is wrong because what you are thinking represents your concept of that person at the moment; and that concept changes from moment to moment and from year to year.

You must learn not to hate or fear your concept of life, whether it is a concept of humanity, of sin, or of disease, because it is only a concept. There is no real power in concepts. What you are considering as person is not person: it is a concept of a person. But that concept has no power. All power is in God. For example, whatever your concept of me may be, there is no power in it that can touch me. If you think I am good, it makes no difference to me. If you think I am bad, it makes no difference. Your thinking has no power over me. God maintains and sustains me, and I am not subject to anything but God. There is no life in your concept of me. Life is in me, not in your concept of me.

It is much the same about everything you see, hear, touch, taste, or smell: you never really know what it is. A diamond may be beautiful and it may be valuable. Whatever beauty and value there is, however, is in the diamond, not in your opinion of it. You may think it is a rhinestone, but your thinking has not touched the value of the diamond. You have not changed it or its quality. You may think it is perfect, and it may be imperfect. You may think it is imperfect when it is perfect. Yet it is what it is, and the value is in it, not in your concept of it. Out-of-doors there may be sunshine or rain. All the thoughts you think about the sun or the rain have no effect on either one.

The application of this truth to healing work is important. You do not know what a disease or a sin is. You have only a concept of it, and there is no real power in that concept. Furthermore, you do not know the person coming to you for help. You have only a concept of him. There is no real power in your concept; the power is within himself, and that is the power of God because there is no other power.

Recall the Master's statement to Pilate, "Thou couldest have no power at all against me, except it were given thee from above."[1] Now let us look at the facts. Pilate was the governor, endowed with complete authority by Caesar. He was judge and jury. That was the appearance. Yet the Master denied Pilate had any power except what came from the Father. That is exactly what I am saying here. Man has no power to be just or unjust, good or bad, sinful or pure, sick or well because all power is in God and comes forth from the Father within.

The moment you begin to perceive that point, you begin to withdraw power from concepts of forms, persons, and conditions. You do this consciously. There is no power outside of you that can do it for you. It is you, yourself, who must learn to look at a person as the Master looked at Pilate and recognize, "Oh, no, I see now that what I am seeing as you is a concept, an image, an effect; but the power is in God, who made you. Even your thoughts do not have power. It is the God who makes your thoughts who has power. You have no power. All power is in God."

You learn to do the same thing with disease, sin, or lack. You do not just close your eyes and say, "There is no such thing" or "There is no reality in it." That is like the ostrich burying its head in the sand. By ignoring a thing, you cannot change yourself or the thing. You have to be willing to look any form of error right in the eye–any form, no matter how ugly its appearance or how nasty it is. Look right straight at it with the conviction, "You have no power. The power is in the God who directs you, moves you, is your mind, is your Soul, is your Spirit, gave you life, and gave you mind." So you look at a condition and ask, "Where did you come from? You are an effect; you are not a cause. Something produced you. Whatever produced you is the power. And what could have produced you if God made all that was made and nothing was made except what God made?"

GOD ALONE IS POWER

How can there be an infinite God, good, and a disease? Everything is made in God's image and likeness, so even when you are looking at what the world calls disease, you are not looking at disease any more than you are looking at water when you see the water on the desert: you are looking at an image, a mirage, an illusion, an appearance that has no power. It is in that realization that healing takes place—not in denying it, turning away from it, or trying to rise above it but in looking right at it and saying, "God made all that was made, and all that God made is good. Anything God did not make was not made. So whatever you are, you have no power."

In the second and third chapters of Genesis is the account of man's concept of creation, not God's creation. Man looks at that creation with his limited vision and endows it with qualities in accordance with his concept of it. He says, "You are a snake, and I fear you." From then on he lives in fear of a snake. But a few rare people in the world remember that God must have made the snake, too. The snake is never poisoned by snake poison. It is full of it, but it is not poisoned by it; so evidently, it is poison only when we accept the concept of it as poison. As a matter of fact, snake venom is extracted and used for medicinal purposes. It is a strange world: we fear a snakebite; and yet a doctor takes the substance considered poisonous, injects it into a person, and helps or heals certain physical disorders.

It is all a matter of concept. What you see, hear, taste, touch, and smell is not God's creation; it is a concept of God's creation. There is no power in it except the power belief gives it. There is in reality no power in anything you can think about, see, hear, taste, touch, or smell. All power is in God. As you persist in that, as an activity of consciousness day in and day out, it becomes a matter of conviction.

RIGHTEOUS JUDGMENT

The Master taught his disciples to turn away from judgments of persons and things when he said, "Why callest thou me good? There is none good but one, that is, God."[2] If you are not to call Jesus good, then do not call any person or any thing good. Do not call health good; do not call wealth good; do not call happiness good; call only God good. Do not ever call any effect good because the good is in the cause.

It is just as erroneous to look at anything and call it bad. It is not good and it is not bad. It has no good power and it has no bad power because all power is in God. The moment you can take good power and bad power out of an effect, you have obeyed Jesus' teaching on two points. You are not calling a person good; you are calling God good. And you are not fearing the evil of Pilate because you are recognizing God as the only power. So you have removed good and evil from effect, and now you have all power in God.

There is no way of judging righteous judgment by appearances. Do not look at what appears to be a good condition and judge it to be good because it is not. Its only goodness is in God. Do not look at any evil and call it evil because that is judging only by appearances. You have no knowledge of what lies behind appearances, so it is a matter of training yourself to be able to

look at human appearances of both good and evil and
say, "Neither do I judge you. Neither do I declare you
to be good or evil. I will say you must be spiritual
because God created all that is, and God is Spirit." This
last point is very important because Infinite Way
healing is practiced on this basis.

It is possible for someone to pass a medical examina-
tion for insurance one day and die of heart disease the
next week. The doctor had judged from appearances.
According to all tests, there was normal functioning and
none of the instruments detected the discord. Doctors
have told many people they will soon die and yet they
are still alive and the doctor is dead. A doctor's verdict
may be that a person has only another week or a month
to live, but the doctor does not know what is going on
in the patient's consciousness that is operating to defeat
the doctor's judgment. There are forces at work that
doctors know nothing about. There are forces at work
that you and I know nothing about or we know too
little; so there is no use judging by appearances.

A person may be dying of disease today and have life
whole and complete tomorrow. It is not a question of
what conclusion you or I reach when we judge by
appearances only. If we want to judge righteous judgment, the truth is this: God is life, so life is eternal. That
is the truth. But if I were to say you are in good health
or in bad health today, or you have integrity or you do
not have integrity today, I would be judging by appearances. I do not know the reality of you; I know only the
appearance you are presenting.

By withholding judgment, by neither judging nor
condemning you, I realize I know nothing about you
except that you are God appearing as individual being.

I do not know if you are good or bad, sick or well; but I know you are God appearing, and on that I stand. All that God is, you are. All that God has, you have. God constitutes your being. I cannot see that with my eyes. With my eyes, I can judge only by appearances. I could even judge how old you are and how many years you have left to walk on earth, but I could do that only with my human judgment. Then you might turn around and fool me.

It is not possible to make a correct judgment by looking at appearances because you are what you are; and what you are is God manifest, God expressed, God being, Christhood. You are Spirit; but I do not know what Spirit is, so I am not engaging in any judgment. I am just making the declaration of *is*.

I do not know what Spirit is, so I still have no judgment as to what you are. You do not know what Spirit is either. You do not know what Soul is; you do not know what Consciousness is. So the moment I say, "You are Soul," I am saying you are what you are; and I do not know what it is, even though the appearance may be that you are good or bad, sick or well, short or tall. I only know you are Soul, Spirit, and life. That is having no condemnation, criticism, judgment, praise, or flattery. That is just stating the truth. The moment I qualify that and say you are good, bad, rich, poor, healthy, sick, young, or old, I am in the realm of judgment, of concepts, and of appearances; and I will make no progress that way.

Do not try to understand what God is with the mind because there is no way to do that. Once you get to that silent place at the center of your being, God will reveal Itself; but you will never be able to put It into words, even after you experience It. So there is no use trying to think about It with the mind. Do not try to think of what man is because you will never figure that one out either. Man is the son of God, and you do not know what the son of God is. Man in his true identity is the Christ, and you do not know what the Christ is because the spiritual sonship of man never reveals itself to human identity.

DOMINION OVER YOUR CONCEPTS

God gave dominion to the man in the first chapter of Genesis who was made in God's image and likeness. A human being was never given dominion, but the man made in God's image and likeness is the man you are when you stop accepting appearances. You are the image and likeness of God only when you stop having concepts, when you stop having opinions or beliefs about this universe and instead listen for a spiritual impartation. Then your mind is entirely free of any opinions or judgments, and you are the child of God. All that the Father has is pouring itself through to you.

God does not impart Itself to human beings. If God did, there would not be a sick or a sinful person; there would not be an accident; there would not be a war. Humanhood is something separate and apart from God, or it would not be in trouble. God appearing as man is not in trouble, is not dying, is not poor, or is not on a battlefield. You are that spiritual man only when you have learned to stop thinking in terms of good and evil. That is when you are God Itself in expression. When you are labeling nobody and no condition as either good or evil, you are the child of God; and you have dominion over everything.

Everything is concept. Everything that exists on earth is a concept. Because you really are God appearing as individual being, I have no control over you. But if I am entertaining a human concept about you as being young or old, rich or poor, sick or well, I can have dominion over that concept of you; and the moment I have attained dominion over my concept of you, I behold you as you are and I am satisfied with that likeness. You have not been changed because you were the child of God all the time. All that has changed is my concept of you, and that is what constitutes healing.

Spiritually, no person has dominion over any other person. God never gave one person power over another, even for good. Judging righteous judgment gives you dominion over your concept. Righteous judgment is understanding that God is the reality of individual being. Knowing that, you have not changed an individual. You have changed your concept of the individual; you have withdrawn judgment. Now you know who the individual is: Christ, the child of God. This is having dominion over your concept.

The concept of disease is that even insignificant ailments can become serious or fatal. The concept of germs is that they are carriers of infection or contagion. Now exercise your dominion and say, "Wait a minute! Let's look at these little fellows. Who made you? If you were made at all, God made you. If you have any life at all, it is God-life. If you have any intelligence at all, it is God-intelligence. You have no power: you are an effect; you are a concept. I am not going to judge by appearances: I am going to judge righteous judgment. And what is righteous judgment? All power is in God."

You have done nothing to the germ; you have exercised your dominion over the *concept* of germs. That germ goes merrily along, but it does not hurt or harm anybody. All those who have been in healing work have witnessed healings of infections and contagious diseases. Some have even helped to stop the spread of infection and contagion during epidemics and have proved that the idea of infection or contagion is only a concept.

POWER IN CAUSE, NOT EFFECT

You do not judge, you do not condemn. You "judge righteous judgment."[3] You look at the condition: "Well, here you are, effects. That settles it right there. If you are an effect, you cannot be a cause. And if you are an effect, you cannot have power."

Your body is an effect. Knowing that, you will stop believing your body can become sick or old. Of its own accord, it has to stay the way it is forever. It cannot move; it has no intelligence; it has no desire to go to the right, left, up, or down. It remains where it is forever until you move it.

If, however, you accept the belief that your body is subject to your control—your whims or personal desires—you will sometimes have a pure body and sometimes a sinful one, sometimes a healthy one and sometimes a sick one, sometimes a young one and sometimes an old one. But if you recognize that all power is God-power operating as your consciousness, your body will be subject only to God, divine Intelligence; and it will be God-governed and maintained.

Think of your heart. It cannot stop or start itself. There is Something that acts upon it and makes it function. That Something we call God. The minute you believe you have power to make your heart start or stop, your heart will fluctuate in accordance with your desires of any given moment. Instead of believing that, give your heart back to God and do the same thing with all the rest of the organs and functions of your body. Understand that God made you in His image and likeness and that your body is the temple of the living God. It is God-governed and God-controlled.

You can have healings through a practitioner or teacher, but the day ultimately must come when you assume the responsibility to maintain a conscious awareness of God-government. The only way you can do this is to see that everything that exists as visible form exists at the standpoint of effect. All else is God, which is invisible. Anything visible—whether you can see it, hear it, taste it, touch it, or smell it—exists as effect, and there is no power in effect. All power is in Cause. Do not hate the effect; do not fear it; and do not unduly love it. If it is something on your level of goodness, enjoy it. Do not love it, but remember that the part you are enjoying is of God.

Never be too joyous about a physical healing or the evidence of supply. Be joyous about the realization of Spirit that manifested Itself as healing or as supply. Keep your joy in God and not in effect. Otherwise, you will be like the eccentric millionaire who had three million dollars and yet was afraid to spend fifteen cents for lunch. That is what comes of putting power in effect. Life is in God; love is in God; satisfaction is in God; peace is in God; happiness is in God; supply is in God. It is only as people go out and try to find these things in persons, in dollars, or in mansions that they lose their way.

DO NOT TRY TO BECOME FREE
OF PERSONS OR CONDITIONS

Healing is all based on not judging by appearances, not putting value in concepts, but in every case realizing, "You are an effect and you have no power." Never try to become free from anyone or anything. No person in reality has any power, and this truth will be your freedom. You will not be free *from* anything or anybody, but you will be free the very minute you know there never was power in a condition, a circumstance, or a person. Then you will find yourself as free as you are free from the water on the desert once you know it is not water but only a mirage.

When you are free from the mirage on the desert, you have not become free from water because there was no water there. So it is when you discover you are free from person or condition; it is not really true because there never was a menacing or dangerous person or condition there. You are free now from a mirage, from a belief that there is a power, a person, or a presence outside of God. Every person is the presence of God because God is present as person, as individual you or me.

You are not separate and apart from God and, through this work, going to get back to God. Through this work, you are going to awaken out of the dream that there can be any separation. If you have been dreaming you are drowning in the ocean, awakening does not take the water away from you; and it does not take you out of the ocean. It reveals to you that you are in bed. So this work never takes you out of sin, disease, or lack. It wakes you up, and then you look around and realize you are in heaven. You have been there all the time, dreaming you were in hell.

As long as you are seeing a person or a condition as having power and are judging good and evil, you are in the dream. The moment you can withdraw your judgment and realize, "You are neither good nor evil; you are neither dead nor alive; you are neither rich nor poor: you are Spirit," you are waking up, out of the dream, to the mystical consciousness of oneness. When that realization comes, the dream is no longer there. This is something that must be done individually as well as collectively.

This truth that I am giving you has been revealed throughout the ages many times and in many ways, and it is a truth that will make people free. We could be free of sins, diseases, wars, lacks, and limitations right now if we could be made to accept this truth.

Do Not Try to Change Evil into Good

The things of the earth over which we have dominion are concepts and we do not have dominion out here. Do not try to make it rain or make the sun shine out here; do not try to make somebody well out here; do not try to get somebody employed out here. Whatever is to happen must happen inside your own being, and this change is brought about by your having dominion over your concepts. The moment you have a concept and somewhere in it you find something good or evil, you must work to come to a place where you withdraw your concepts of good and evil.

Do not try to change evil into good because you will just have a different concept; and tomorrow, next week, or next month it will be back on the evil side again. Do not be happy with a good appearance because some day it will fool you and change to a bad appearance. If you look at a thing and see it as evil, your natural reaction is to want to see it as good. What you must do is look at it and not see it as good, but see it as Spirit; neither good nor bad.

No one knows what Spirit is. No matter what you think you know, it is not true; and the sooner you begin to understand that, the better off you will be. You have no understanding, and you never will have. It is God who has infinite understanding, and you turn within and let God's understanding be revealed to you. Be satisfied with that; and above all, learn it is just as erroneous to label a thing good as it is to label it bad.

LETTING WHAT IS REVEAL ITSELF

It would be a simple matter for me to judge humanly what you are, who you are, or how you are. But that would be wrong because that would be my concept of you, and it still would not be you. This all began to reveal itself to me when I was sitting at the breakfast table one morning with a student. We were having a discussion about not praying to God because there is no way to get anything from God and there is no way to get God to change anything, so praying to God for something is futile. At that point, I saw on our table a little jug of maple syrup and I said, "What is it?"

His answer was, "Maple syrup."

"How do you know?"

"It is an association of ideas. They serve hot cakes, and they always have syrup around."

By his answer, it was plain he was judging it was maple syrup. I said, "That's your opinion. That's your concept. But suppose we opened it and found it was not maple syrup but some other syrup. Maybe it is not even syrup. What about that?"

"Well, that could be true, too. I was just judging by the fact that that is what you would expect it to be."

I continued, "Now, how about our withdrawing an opinion as to whether it is maple syrup or even if it is something good or something bad and just declaring it is, not what it is. It just is. Something is there, that is evident. Something is there, but I do not know whether it is good or bad. I can judge by appearances and say it is maple syrup and therefore it is good; but somebody else could say it is maple syrup, and he does not like it. So to him it would still be maple syrup, but it would be bad. But on the other hand, when you tasted it, it might not be maple syrup at all; so we could be wrong on every count. One thing we can say with certainty: it is. Something is there."

That is exactly what I do with healing work. You present yourself or your condition to me, and frankly I know nothing about you or the condition. I am sure I know less about anatomy than almost anybody in the world, and I certainly know less about all those things that make up what the world calls its ills. But you present yourself to me with your problem, and I turn within and all I know is, *IS*. "Something is here. Now, Father, You define it."

An awareness usually comes, which is just the same as if it said, " 'This is my beloved Son, in whom I am well pleased.'[4] Do not malpractice him." The moment I have the conviction within that you are the child of

God, that there is nothing present here but the presence of God, and that there is no power here but the power of God, healing will take place.

Spiritual healing consists of being able to face the world without an opinion of good or evil, retiring within and asking, "Father, what is this?" Then the Father may remind you, "This is my beloved child in whom I am well pleased." Or the Father will say, "This is the presence of God;" "This is the power of God;" or "This is nothing separate and apart from God." It does not always come in words like that, but it comes in the conviction or awareness of the omnipresence of God and God alone.

You meet people you like. No words are exchanged; you do not say, "I like you" or "You like me." You just have the awareness of a mutuality. Rarely does anyone voice such thoughts, but there is a mutuality and an understanding without any words. So it is in healing. God may occasionally speak to you in an audible voice, but that is rare. Most of the time it comes as a conviction, and you abide in the conviction that all is well. This comes with your ability to have no labels as to good or evil. You cannot judge righteous judgment because righteous judgment comes from God, and it can come only in the degree that you are listening. In your inner silence, you must be listening to God and you will either hear audibly, feel, sense, or become aware of God; and that is all that is necessary.

Only be careful that you do not prejudge something as evil and then turn to God for help. God is omnipresent, so there is not use in going to God to get God to be present. There is no use in going to God to get God to be good to you. There is no use in going to God to get

God's power because God is right here with all his power. God is present where you are. God is the omnipresent power of good. God's grace is sufficient. God's grace is not something you can get. God's grace is something that *is*. God governs this universe by grace, not by law, not by desire, not by will, but by grace. God's grace is omnipresent in your consciousness.

A basic principle of The Infinite Way is found in the word *IS*. God is; harmony is; life is; love is; peace is; joy is; power is; dominion is because God is. God is infinite, omnipresent, omnipotent, and omniscient. Do not turn to God for anything. Be still and let God reveal Itself within you because God is already eagerly waiting to reveal Itself. It is no use seeking God. All you have to do is to inherit It. You do not work for It; you do not deserve It; you do not labor by the sweat of your brow for It. God already is. God already is fulfillment. God already is completeness. Why should you want anything else?

~ 8 ~

ATTAINING DOMINION THROUGH *I*

THE secret of harmonious existence lies in attaining a consciousness of that Grace within every person awaiting recognition. Whether or not one recognizes and demonstrates it in this lifetime, the next, or the one after is an individual affair, depending on one's spiritual growth or lack of it.

Some of you may be bored with the repetition that is about to begin. Instead of saying, "Oh, I know that. I have done that," forget your past experience with it; begin as if it were something entirely new; and do it faithfully. Do not do it with half a mind, as if you already knew what was coming. Do it with your full attention because this is the only way of imparting The Infinite Way principles to you.

Look down at your feet, very attentively, and ask yourself, "Am I down there in those feet? Do those feet constitute me, or are they mine?" Do this very slowly because otherwise you will not have the experience. Are you down there in those feet? Do you think you live there, or are those feet yours, yours to command, yours to order, yours to direct?

Now travel up to your knees, and look at yourself from the knees down to the toenails with the same

123

question, "Am I to be found down there? Is this I, or are
these mine?" Go on up to your waist. Are you there, or
is all this yours? Can you not move it at your will? From
there, travel up to the neck; but be a little bit more
thorough and examine that area of the body between
the neck and the waist, front and back, outside and
inside. Look inside and ask yourself, "Is this I? This is
what I see in the mirror, but is this I or is this mine?
Was not this body given to me for many uses?"

From the neck, continue right up to the topmost hair
of your head; and be sure to look around inside your
head and notice your brain and your ears. Look down
through your throat and see if you can find yourself any
place in your body. Look behind your eyes, because
sometimes we think we are behind our eyes looking out,
and see if you can find yourself even there. Eventually,
if you do this faithfully, you must conclude you are not
anywhere within your body.

If, during this exercise, you have not become fully
convinced, if it is not absolutely clear to you that there
is no place within your body where you are, do it again,
and if necessary, a third or fourth time, until you are no
longer taking my word for it but can bear witness to the
fact that you have searched yourself thoroughly and
know you are not inside that frame. You will not make
spiritual progress until you have come to that realization
because until this dawns on you, you never will know
who you are, what you are, where you are, why you are,
or how you function.

THE BODY, AN INSTRUMENT OF CONSCIOUSNESS

After you have gone through this practice, I would
like you to step about six inches in back of yourself and

about six inches over your head and look down at yourself. The way you do that is to close your eyes and lift yourself up there and say, "I, I." Lift yourself up, look down through the top of your head, and realize, "I."

I am not in that body; therefore, I must be outside that body. If I am outside that body, I can localize myself; and I can be here, there, or anywhere. But I choose now to be right behind my body and above it so I can look down upon this body, I in back of and above the body, looking down upon it. I, who am not in the body, have now localized myself; and as I look at this body, I will ask myself: How can this body function without me? How can this body take a step forward or backward? How can the arms be raised or lowered? Will this body do it of itself?

Can this body, of itself, digest, or am I the activity of the organs of digestion, the same as I am the activity of my hands and feet, my arms and legs? I know I am the activity of my hands and feet; I know my hands cannot give or accept a gift. It is I who accept and I who give, using my hands as an instrument. Can my feet walk, or my legs, or my whole body? I know if I get up from my chair, it is because I, I who am I, choose to get up from this chair; and my body must follow. It has no choice; it cannot refuse. When I am ready to stand up, the body must stand up; and when I am ready to walk, the body must walk because I have been given dominion over this body.

Take several periods to adjust yourself to this attitude of looking down upon yourself and witnessing the helplessness of your arms and legs, your hands and feet, except as you direct them and move them. If you set your body down before the most bountiful meal, your body could not eat it unless you chose to put the body through the motions of getting the food and drink into your system. Remember, it is you who are doing all this; and you are doing it for yourself because you were given God-given dominion over your life and over your body. You can choose whether you will sow to the flesh or to the Spirit. The choice is with you.

CONSCIOUSNESS UNFOLDING

Although you call yourself "I," this does not fully identify you because you may not know the nature of the *I* that you are. In order to gain some idea of what you are, imagine for a moment you had never learned to read. Try to think of what your life would be without the ability to read. You would know nothing of what is in the newspapers; you would know nothing of what is in travel books; you would know nothing of any part of the world except where you are or what you can see on television or hear on the radio. You could not read either the Bible or philosophy, so you would know nothing of the world's philosophies or religions. With this limitation, your mind would be rather small. Your outlook on life would be exceedingly narrow. Think of all the things you would not know, all you would not know that you did not know. As far as you are concerned, your little neighborhood would be all there is.

You can see trees and flowers, so you know them. But because you realize that you do at least recognize trees, grass, flowers, and food and that you do recognize forests, streets, and cities, you now realize that the "I" as which you identify yourself must be a state of awareness, for at least that I is aware. It may not be aware of very much, but that I is aware. So this I that you are really is awareness. A better word is consciousness: I am consciousness, in this human state, a very insignificant bit of consciousness, but consciousness nevertheless.

To continue with this example, someone tells you what it means to be able to read; so you decide to learn to read. You become aware of words like "beautiful," "magnificent," "inspiring," and "grandeur" as you continue learning to read. Through the newspaper, you learn what is happening in an adjoining city or state. Eventually, you learn what is happening in foreign countries. This is your consciousness expanding. No, it is not that at all. The consciousness you are is infinite; so even in this state of ignorance or unawareness, you can now begin to read and become aware of a wider horizon.

The consciousness you are is infinite, and you are taking in more and more of the great *IS*, of the great universe. Someday this awareness will expand; so even though you can see only the horizon, you will know the horizon is not there in spite of the limitations of eyesight.

BECOMING AWARE OF THE INFINITE NATURE
OF INDIVIDUAL BEING

From now on, so many things happen to you that you cannot keep pace with them; and you are becoming more and more aware of the infinite nature of your being. Soon you learn you have control over your entire body; and eventually more and more of the nature of your dominion over everything between the sky and the earth becomes apparent to you.

But you will not be growing. You will never be more or less than the *I* that you are. You are consciousness and you are infinite; but you are now emerging from the prodigal state and becoming more and more aware of the infinite nature of your own being and dominion because this *I* that you declare yourself to be is actually consciousness, and the nature of your consciousness is infinity. Someday you will learn why.

"I and my Father are one."[1] Therefore, all that God is, I am; all that the Father has is mine, all within my consciousness. Thus, day by day, I am becoming more aware of what is already within my consciousness and always was there awaiting my recognition. On the Mount of Transfiguration, the Master showed three of his disciples that the ancient Hebrew prophets who had died centuries before were still alive, that they were right there where he was. The truth is they are here where we are. And where are we? In consciousness. Where are you? In my consciousness. Where am I? In your consciousness.

The only place you can keep the message of The Infinite Way is in your consciousness. This message was in your consciousness thousands of years ago, "before Abraham was."[2] But you are only now becoming aware of it, just like our nonreader became aware of reading and through reading became aware of the world of art, literature, music, philosophy, and religion. If he were not infinite consciousness, how could he have become aware of the infinite universe and of the infinity of stars and planets? This consciousness, the consciousness he is, is so infinite that if he set out to learn all the languages in the world, he could. If he set out to embrace all the religions and all the philosophies, he could.

There is nothing he could set himself to do that he could not accomplish because there is no limitation to the consciousness he is, to the *I AM.*

Go back up there now, six inches behind your body and six inches above your head, and look down at your body again. Realize you are not in this body: this body is within your consciousness. Just as the Bible or The Infinite Way books are within your consciousness, so this body is within your consciousness. With that understanding, try to see why the Master could say to the crippled man, "Take up thy bed."[3] I do not know if he said "bed" or "body." I think it more than likely he said "body." Perhaps he said, "Take up your body and walk. You are not in that body, and that body is not holding you in bondage. The body is within you, but you do not know your dominion."

With all your studying, practice, and meditation, you should be at the point where you recognize, "I am not in this body. This body was not given dominion over me. I was given dominion over this body." There can be no limitation if you recognize that as *I,* as this infinite Consciousness, you are given dominion.

LIFTING POWER ABOVE ORGANS AND FUNCTIONS TO *I*

You have been told that when you eat food, the digestive organs go to work and begin digesting, assimilating, transmuting, and eliminating. Look down into your digestive organs and prove to yourself that is not true; your digestive organs cannot do a thing until *I* within you begin to digest. *I* digest my food; *I* assimilate my food—not the digestive organs, but *I.*

You do not go to a doctor or a practitioner and say, "My digestive organs do not operate." You say, "I am

not digesting my food." That is about the truth of it.
You are not digesting properly because you have given
over the dominion of digestion to your digestive organs
instead of learning to sit up behind yourself, look down,
and say, "I was given dominion over this body; this
body was not given dominion over me!"

We are told the heart is a pumping station for the
whole blood system. It takes the blood in and sends it
out again. But now look down from where you are and
see if that is true. See if it is not *I*, and see if the heart
could function without *I*. A corpse cannot do this
because the *I* is gone. The heart cannot do it of itself,
there must be consciousness. God gave man dominion
over the heart, the liver, and the lungs.

Because nothing can happen except through an
activity of your consciousness, consciously withdraw
any power you have heretofore ignorantly given to your
body and lift it up into the *I* that you are. Let yourself
be governed by that "I AM THAT I AM."[4] Let your
body be governed by that *I* and stop acknowledging that
you are weak: *I* is never weak. If the body is, it is
because you have relinquished dominion over it.

"And I, if I be lifted up from the earth, will draw all
men unto me."[5] If I lift up the *I* of me, I can lift up
every organ and function of the body unto that *I*.
Consciousness has infinite forms and activities, and
some of these I must consciously utilize. For instance, I
must consciously decide to walk, to talk, to run, to get
up, to sit down, to eat, or not to eat. But there is another
activity of consciousness to which the functions of the
body have been given so you do not have to say to your
digestive organs, "Digest." You do not have to say to the
eliminative organs, "Eliminate." You do not have to say

to the heart, "Function." All you must do is know these activities of the body are really not activities of the body, they are activities of consciousness; and let them perform their work.

We all have been in bondage because we have allowed the organs and the functions of the body to accept the medical belief that they can do what they want to do and can control us, instead of understanding that the organs and functions of the body are actually animated and motivated by consciousness. Therefore, I can restore to *I*, my individual consciousness, the activity of my body and of those functions of my body that are not consciously controlled.

Instead of asking, "How is the heart beating? How are the digestive organs working? How is the liver functioning?" lift up every activity of the organs of the body into consciousness and restore the dominion to consciousness. Then say, "Now, consciousness, function." As often as it may be necessary and as long as the body is not fully responding, repeat this. Lift up the activity of the organs into consciousness and say, "Now, consciousness, take over." It will not be long before you discover your body is meant to function through your consciousness. Your consciousness was given the dominion over these internal organs and functions and muscles, but we have failed to exercise that dominion, mainly because we thought we were in the body and had no dominion over it.

CONSCIOUSNESS

What I am explaining about the body is used only as an illustration or symbol of the greater thing. If you understand this much, the rest will become clear to you. Here I am; I am consciousness, and consciousness is infinite. There is an area of consciousness with dominion over every facet of my life. My supply is not at the mercy of "man, whose breath is in his nostrils."[6] God intended me to have infinite supply, all I need and twelve baskets full left over. But God did not put me at the mercy of anybody's whim or will, generosity or lack of it. God provided an activity of my consciousness to bring my supply to me or to unfold as my supply. Just as there is an area of my consciousness that governs the organs and functions of my body, so there is an area of my consciousness that governs my supply. Therefore, I can acknowledge, "I have hidden manna. I have meat the world knows not of," because there is an activity of my consciousness that has dominion over my supply.

There is an activity or function of your consciousness that is to bring to you your own. There are words in John Burrough's poem "Waiting," that could confound the very elect if they were not spiritually wise: "My own shall come to me." If you think about that, you will probably say to yourself, "Mr. Burroughs, you must be mistaken. I know about a million people in the world whose own is not coming to them, maybe two or three million. Yet your poem sounds so beautiful." It is beautiful; and it is true, if you know what John Burroughs knew, that there is an area of your consciousness, a hidden manna within you, that goes before you and brings to you your own: your companionship, those of your own household, those of your spiritual household, those with whom you can commune on various levels of human and spiritual existence. Your consciousness is infinite. It has infinite faculties, infinite activities, and infinite functions; one of those is to draw to you those you can bless and who in turn can bless you.

If you look at yourself in the mirror and believe you are seeing your Self, you are going to be like the person who cannot read. All you will be aware of is your limitation. Instead, say the word, "*I*," and get up there outside of yourself. Look down and say, "Hands, you cannot move if I do not move you. Feet, you cannot move if I do not move you. Teeth, you cannot chew if I do not chew." You have to become aware of the *I*. Raise up the *I* of your own being: "I, if I be lifted up." Lift up that *I* in you.

Lift up the child of God in you with the word *I*. Get up there and let your shoulders go back as you look down and realize,

I and the Father are one, and the Father has given me dominion over this body and over my business. I do not need to hypnotize anybody into buying my product; I do not need to think about how to get employment. I need to know the truth! There is an activity of my consciousness that is going out before me now, taking care of my employment or anything else that may be necessary to my functioning.

The only way you can agree with this is by believing there is an infinite, divine, creative Principle, which at the same time is infinite Intelligence. Everything and everybody created by that Principle was created for a specific purpose. If you do not believe that, you cannot be helped. If you do believe that, you cannot be unemployed because God cannot have a wasted action, idea, thought, or projection.

If there is a divine idea, it came from God; and God will see it is fulfilled. Therefore, you must never try to dominate anyone. Never permit your thought to extend outside yourself as if to govern, control, or influence any more than you now realize you cannot influence God. Your life is lived within the infinite boundaries of your own consciousness, and your way of life is knowing the truth.

As I sit here knowing this truth—and really I am not sitting in a chair, I am up there where I told you to be—I am not telling my heart, liver, lungs, or blood what to do. I am knowing the truth that the activity or the functioning of every organ of my body is in consciousness, consciousness governing every part of it. Because I, Consciousness, am infinite, there is an area or activity of my consciousness responsible for the success of my business activity, for its spiritual fruitage, for income and outgo.

You all know the limitations and the difficulties of family life, more especially when everyone is not united on the spiritual path. But there is an area of your consciousness that governs your family life. You have only to remember the rule given by the Master: "Therefore all things whatsoever ye would that men should do to you, do ye even so to them."[7] All you can do to bring about harmonious relationships is to love your friends, your relatives, and your enemies.

There is an area of consciousness, an activity and a function of your consciousness, that is to go before you and make smooth your family relationships. There is an area, an activity, and a function of your consciousness that is a divine spiritual Presence that goes before you to make the "crooked"[8] places straight, to prepare "mansions"[9] for you, and to be the cement of your human relationships.

If you must drive on the road, there is an activity of your consciousness that goes before you to keep everyone in his rightful lane, to see that everyone is functioning according to divine law and order. You do not have to think about it. You merely must know the truth that the government of the automobiles on the road is not in the hands of a police department that often is not there: it is in the hands of the infinite Consciousness, which you are.

In every facet of your life, in every facet of your human experience, you have a secret and very sacred word within yourself: "I have meat the world knows not of. I have hidden manna." All you do is to rest back in that and *let* that go before you. The only thing necessary to keep it functioning is to live a life of integrity.

~9~

THE MYSTIC AND HEALING

MANY persons wonder if attaining the awareness of God makes one an instrument for healing. There is no categorical answer to this question. Attainment of awareness may bring forth a healing consciousness, but it does not necessarily do so. If the awareness attained is deep enough, it can be a mystical experience, which means conscious union or a conscious at-onement with God; but even that does not always enable a person to do healing work.

The healing consciousness is the consciousness that has the spiritual discernment to see through "this world" to "My kingdom." This discernment or ability to perceive Reality is not reserved for those who have had mystical illumination. It is possible for almost anyone who is willing to become a student of spiritual truth to attain a measure of spiritual discernment. There are those who achieve it in one day; there are those who achieve it in a few weeks or a few months; and there are others who work for years to achieve it. One deciding factor in the length of time it takes to develop this awareness is the desire for it.

Spiritual discernment is not to be had for spare change or spare time. It requires a greater devotion than would be necessary in trying to learn a new language or to play a musical instrument. There must be the desire of the heart. Given that, and the willingness to study and practice, it will be only a short time before a person can achieve some measure of spiritual awareness and show it in actual work.

THE DEARTH OF SPIRITUAL HEALING

It should surprise everyone that more religious leaders are not doing spiritual healing work because there can be no question but that the vast majority of them are honest and sincere lovers of God, seekers of God who live their life close to God, at least as close to God as their understanding permits. That, in most cases, is in a great measure. If God, as God is usually understood, were a healer of disease, why in these hundreds of years since the Bible has been in existence have these dedicated religious leaders not gained a monopoly on spiritual healing? Their life is lived in God and dedicated to the service of God and man; they are earnest, honest, and sincere. They are not doing more spiritual healing work because, in spite of the recognition of the omnipotence of God, power is still being given to sin, disease, death, lack, and limitation. They believe disease is permanent and real and they accept the premise that they can pray to God to remove it.

If God could remove disease, no one would have to pray for its removal. Healing is not based on the premise that there is a disease, a God that can heal it, and a certain man or woman or a group of men or women who must bring God into the picture and gain God's good will. In the kingdom of God, there is no disease.

God maintains and sustains Its kingdom intact, harmonious, healthful, complete, perfect, spiritual, and whole.

Jesus Christ and others like him have been instruments of God in revealing to the world that disease, sin, and death are no part of God's kingdom, are not real, and cannot stand in the face of that understanding. When you touch the hem of the spiritual Robe, you will understand that in the entire kingdom of God there is not a sinner or a diseased person.

Healing has to do with your individual state of consciousness, a state of consciousness that apprehends the idea of God as infinite Spirit and therefore of a universe, including man, infinitely and eternally spiritual. What appears to this world as sin, disease, lack, and limitation does not partake of the nature of the real and has no law, cause, effect, substance, or reality. Then with your thoughts centered on God and Reality, listening, being ever alert for that divine Impulse to assure you God is on the field, will healings take place.

There have been many mystics in the history of the world; and although some of them did come into the awareness of the truth that what we call material existence represents but the illusion of the five senses, the belief of good and evil was deeply ingrained in most of them. When it was revealed to Gautama the Buddha that "this world" is *maya*, or illusion, his illumination was so great that he instantly knew there is a divine spiritual creation here and now but that the universal concept of it is illusory. With that understanding, he did great healing work.

Eventually, Buddha's revelation was corrupted, and the word *maya* came to mean the opposite of God. His later followers were left once again with two powers: the power of Reality to overcome the power of illusion. But illusion cannot be overcome. When you understand a thing is illusion, you are done with it. It has no more existence. It had existence only while you thought it existed, but when you saw it as illusion, that was the end of it.

Today the term "mortal mind" or "carnal mind" is used to signify the nothingness of this world of appearance. But again it came to be set up as a power opposed to God, and the struggle was on. You cannot do healing work if you believe there are entities with which God has to contend, battle, or overcome. That is setting up a power apart from God. It is necessary to get back to the original revelation of the great mystics that there is but one power and that everything embraced in the term illusion is a nothingness. When you perceive that, you have a healing consciousness.

The belief in good and evil is what maintains humanhood. In the degree that you lose your belief in good and evil, however, you are no longer human: you are spiritual. That is when you have a healing consciousness. Then you are not as subject to the human errors or limitations in life as you were when you were entertaining both good and evil. To some extent, you have become immune to the claims of the world, but not one hundred percent. When you attain that one hundred percent, you can no longer mingle with others; and life becomes too burdensome living with the human mind. It is then that the mystics who have attained a real and complete sense of neither good nor evil retire from the world. They no longer want to be a part of it.

LIMITATION, THE FRUITAGE OF THE
PAIRS OF OPPOSITES

There is no lack in God's kingdom. The only lack is in man's kingdom, and that is because he has abundance *and* lack: he has good *and* evil, up *and* down, in *and* out, black *and* white. That is why he experiences limitation. The moment an individual begins to perceive there is only God and that God's infinity precludes any evil, he has no further problems of lack.

From the moment a person realizes even in a measure, "Thank You, Father, I am one with You, and all that You have is mine. I am not dependent on 'man, whose breath is in his nostrils.'[1] I am not dependent on earning my living by the sweat of my brow," he begins to be picked up by an invisible Presence. Supply opens in the most normal and natural ways, without taking thought, without fighting, without arguing, without suing.

You may have a mystical experience and you may have a great deal of sickness and poverty; but if you do, it is only because you are still embracing the idea of God as a power over evil. In doing that, you are holding yourself in the dream. If you relax and let go, stop thinking, and just enjoy that inner communion with God, agreeing there is no power apart from God, you will be picked up by this inner Thing called the Christ, the Spirit of God in man, or the Holy Ghost; and you will understand why Paul could say, "I live; yet not I, but Christ liveth in me."[2] . . . "I can do all things through Christ which strengtheneth me."[3]

Nobody ever need fear passing on while he is devoting himself to a spiritual activity because the only thing to which he can pass on is greater and greater glory. That which carried him through this experience carries him on to the next plane, the next plane, the next plane, and all those to come until there are no more rebirths.

THE SELF-MAINTAINING POWER OF LOVE

What is called the power of God is not really power at all. For example, I do not need any power this minute. I am sitting here in an atmosphere of love, so why do I need a power? I am sitting here in an atmosphere of life, so for what would I need a power? I am sitting here in an atmosphere of joy. I do not need a power for anything. I am content and complete. But there is a Power here. There is a Power that created this atmosphere, that created us in Its image, and that maintains and sustains us. But I need no power. God is here; God is power; God is the power of the atmosphere of my environment; and God will maintain this atmosphere unto eternity if I stand fast in it.

Few mystics knew anything about healing work or ever did any. So far as is known, aside from the realization of *I*, they did not know the nature of God. Except for the Master, most mystics looked upon God as a great Power, contending with or overcoming other powers. No one can heal spiritually until he or she comes to the realization not only that *I* is God, but that besides that *I*, there are no other powers.

The few mystics who caught the fullness of the realization of God as truly infinite in nature could heal. They could say to whatever Pilate was in their experience, "Thou couldest have no power at all against me, except it were given thee from above."[4] This is because in the consciousness of the mystic who can heal, there is the realization not only that *I* is God, but that besides *I* there are no other powers–physical, mental, moral, or financial. No other power can act in, on, or through him.

Isaiah must have had the healing gift because he said, "The Spirit of the Lord God is upon me; because the Lord hath anointed me to preach good tidings unto the meek; he hath sent me to bind up the brokenhearted, to proclaim liberty to the captives."[5] He knew there were no other gods before *Me*. The *I* of his being was the infinity of being, and there were no other powers.

A mystic of that attainment will not say, "Oh, the power of God works through me to heal you" or "God will heal you." He knows God never healed anybody or anything. What would you think of a God who would heal one person and not all persons? The sinners usually have the best record of being healed, while it would appear that God has not healed the countless good men and women on earth.

It is a person's realization that disease is not a power that is responsible for healing. That is why Jesus did not say, "God will heal you." He said, "And ye shall know the truth, and the truth shall make you free."[6] He did not say, "God will forgive you." He said, "Neither do I condemn thee: go, and sin no more."[7]

Most modern mystics like Whitman and Tennyson were not healers because they did not have the vision of God as the Only and the Infinite. They had God and error, too; they had God and something from which God could protect or save people. They had God and something of which God could heal them, but that is not the full mystical awareness of Jesus Christ.

THE TRUTH OF *I AM*

Jesus Christ knew, "I am the bread of life."[8] He also knew *I* am your bread, too. *I* am your supply. He could supply multitudes because he saw no distinction between his purse and their purse. He saw no distinction between his health and their health. He recognized only one person, and that was *I*. Moses understood, "I AM THAT I AM,"[9] and he could heal. Jesus understood *I AM*, and he could heal. Isaiah saw It, and he could heal. When you have the consciousness of *I AM*, you can heal. That is the mystery and the miracle of Infinite Way teaching. It is based not on God as a great Power, but on the universal truth that "I and my Father are one."[10]

When you ask me for help, you will notice that I write or say to you, "*I* am instantly with you." When I say *I* will be with you, I am not saying Joel is going to be with you. What good would it do you if he were? I am saying *I* will be with you. All you have to do is to say, "I." Say it to yourself now. Is it not true that *I* am with you? You have just declared it.

That *I* you have just voiced is God: It is not a person; It is not a man or a woman; It is not somebody with the name of Jones, Brown, or Smith. That *I* is God, and that *I* will never leave you or forsake you. That *I* is a universal *I*. It is the same *I* whether Joel voices It or you voice It. There is only one *I* in all this world, one Ego; and when I say, "*I* am instantly with you," all you have to do to find out if I am telling the truth is say, "I." Say, "*I* am." How much closer could It get to you than that? That is God. That is not a human person talking. That is God. That is the life of your being.

It makes no difference, according to the Psalmist, if you "walk through the valley of the shadow of death"[11]; *I* am there. It makes no difference whether you go up to heaven or down to hell; *I* am there. There is no place you can go where *I* am not. All you have to do is say, *"I,"* or *"I am,"* and you will find *I AM* right there with you.

If you knew the words *I AM,* you could travel to any part of the world and always live in peace, harmony, and prosperity. Keep *I AM* locked up inside of you; start on your journey; and you will reach it, whether it consists of going from your home to your office, into neighboring cities, or around the world.

I am that place where God becomes manifest as individual me. I, the son of God, is right here where I am, joint-heir to all the heavenly riches.

All I have to do is keep that awareness of my true identity and then stop believing it gives me power over error. That is where we lose out in healing, believing we have God-power over error. Error is not a power. *I AM* is the only power:

Thank You, Father, I am. There is no power of sin, no power of disease, no power of lack or limitation. There are no laws of disease, no laws of sin, no laws of lack. There are only laws of abundance, no laws of limitation. All those supposed laws of lack and limitation are man-made creations.

There are degrees of God-realization. There are no degrees of God. That is why in our beginning days in the healing work we may be able to heal the minor claims that come to us but not succeed with the greater ones. We have not yet had a deep enough realization that error is not something to be fought, overcome, risen above, or destroyed. Error is something to be recognized as nothingness. It is no thing; it is no person.

THE PERSON AND THE DISEASE MUST BE NO PART OF YOUR HEALING MEDITATION

When you understand the impersonal nature of error, you begin to do healing work because if you want to heal, you first must get rid of a patient. As long as you have a patient in your mind, you are never going to bring forth healing. As long as you have the name of a disease in your mind, you will not bring forth healing, at least not spiritually. The patient might be healed mentally or by will power, but that is no different from using a plaster or a pill.

To heal spiritually, you instantly drop the person who asks you for help from your thought: his name, identity, and claim. This is because the person is not the claim, and the particular disease is not the claim. The claim is a universal belief of a selfhood apart from God, of an activity apart from God, and of a law apart from God. That is what you are really dealing with.

When somebody named Sue Jones comes along and says, "I am sick," you have to drop Sue Jones and realize, "No, this is not a person. This is the carnal mind. But the carnal mind is not a mind. The carnal mind has no law to support it; it has no substance, no cause, and no reality." Without thinking of the person or her particular claim, you have brought forth a healing by knowing the nothingness of the claim itself.

The claim is the carnal mind, the belief in two powers. You are dealing not with a "he" or a "she," not with a problem; you are dealing with the carnal mind, which is trying to convince you of a life separate and apart from God. The Master said, "Which of you convinceth me of sin?"[12] So who convinces you of a person or a condition apart from God?

With your finite eyes, you can see male and female; you can see old and young. But in my years in this work, I have learned not to look too much at persons but to look through them so I am not often really conscious of who is before me or why. That looses the person's identity in my thought because I am not interested in the person or his or her particular problem except as it presents an opportunity to me to reveal again that God is the only selfhood and that there are no laws except God-made laws.

As long as I do not look upon anyone who comes to me as a sick person to be made well, a sinning person to be reformed, or an unemployed person to be employed, I am on the safe ground of a spiritual healer. If I once take a person into my consciousness as a sick person who should be healed, as a sinner who should be reformed, as a poor person who should have abundance, or as an unemployed person who should be employed, I am back on the level of the mortal dream and I am no longer of any help to the person and will never be of any help to this world. My help is only in proportion as I can impersonalize the entire situation.

There are claims that have to do with persons who are eighty and ninety years of age. Some of you are getting too close to that to believe such numbers mean old age. Do not let anybody convince you of it either.

That suggestion is met in the same way that health and strength of body and mind are preserved: by not accepting anybody who needs healing, reforming, or supplying. You must recognize the only identity to be *I*.

"My glory will I not give to another."[13] If you would say God does not give His glory to disease, age, sin, or lack, where do sin and lack get any glory or power if God is infinite? They have none. They have no glory; they have no law; they have no beauty; they have no continuity because if they do not receive these from God, they do not receive them.

NOT POWER, BUT GRACE

When you sit down to do healing work, all you need is the ability to be quiet and commune with your Father within, realizing that God's grace is infinite. You do not need any power. You are not going to heal anything or anybody. It is an illusion to believe there is anything or anybody to be healed.

Every spiritual healing is proof that sin, disease, and death are not power; so no power is needed to overcome them. When we speak of God as the one Power, do not think of that as a Power you use. Think of It as the Power that created the universe, that maintains it and sustains it; and let It do it while you inwardly commune with It.

It is much as if you were sitting quietly talking to your mother. You do not need any power. God is the only power, and God created this universe through the power of *I*. God maintains it and sustains it. You do not need any power; you need the ability to commune with your inner Self and be at peace with It. Then you will find God is maintaining and sustaining His own creation without any help from you or me.

Would it not be sad if God needed your help or mine? I am afraid we would let Him down too often. We would be asleep or on vacation. I would feel very sorry for God if He were depending on us to help Him—most of us, anyhow. Only a few could live up to it. But God is not dependent on you or me. God does not need our help, not even for each other.

All we need is the same assurance that David had in the Twenty-third Psalm: "The Lord is my shepherd; I shall not want."[14] He did not ask for any God-power. He merely acknowledged, "He maketh me to lie down in green pastures: he leadeth me beside the still waters."[15] It doesn't say a word about my part or my practitioner's part. It just says, "He maketh me to lie down in green pastures." What the Psalmist was doing was contemplating God's goodness within himself.

This is what you have been doing as you have been reading this book. You have been contemplating God as God is functioning in the universe. You have not asked God for any help, and you certainly have not accepted any belief that God needs your help. You have just sat here contemplating the isness of God and of God's creation. You do not make affirmations to make the isness of God true. An affirmation is a statement of what is, but any time you use an affirmation in the hope of making it come true, you are going to get nowhere spiritually. You may accomplish something mentally, but that is different from spiritual healing.

In spiritual healing, you do not address the consciousness of a patient. You do not make a statement of truth to make it come true. If you do, you prevent yourself from doing healing work. You should only make statements of truth of what you already know to be the truth, and then rest in that truth. Too many persons are trying with their mind-power to make it so and then calling it God-healing, spiritual healing, or Christ healing. It is not that at all. Spiritual healing is a realization of what is. By the seeing of your eye or the hearing of your ear, none of this can ever be true because with your eyes and with your ears you will see and hear much of the trouble in the world. Only through spiritual discernment will you see God's government, what the Master called seeing and hearing.

To do spiritual healing, you have to have the inner discernment that sees *I* as the life of individual being and then knows *I* has no age. This *I* was the same when I was born as when I pass on. Youth or age, *I* is always the same. You have to behold that *I* as individual being: *I* am thou; thou art *I*. We are one in Christ Jesus, which means we are one in spiritual sonship. There is only one of us, and I am that one. "Before Abraham was, I am."[16] You cannot detect that with your physical sight or with your physical hearing. That is a matter of inner discernment, and that is the mystical healing consciousness.

~ 10 ~

Dominion Through Daily Realization

THE limitations of our experience are imposed upon us, not by anything we do or do not do or by anything we think or do not think, but by universal belief. Material beliefs have come down to us, not because we knowingly accepted them, not because we knowingly decided we would be as we are, but because subliminally these things were introduced into our consciousness. In other words, things took place in our home, which as children we had no knowledge of seeing or hearing, that registered in our consciousness. In school, things we did not consciously know were going on around us helped to form patterns within us. Prenatal influence, environment, and experiences make up the forces that limit our life experience; and they all are rooted in the universal belief of the ages. Together these things make us the human beings we are. We have the world we have because of these universal beliefs, which have created a materialistic state of consciousness.

We did not choose to be materialistic. Because we were born into a materialistic age, we took on the complexion of material consciousness. All disease, sin, fear, and death itself are imposed upon us. All error has its basis in the universal belief that arises from the acceptance of two powers. On the material level of life, there are two powers; and one is used to overcome another. On the mental level, the power of thought or the power of right thinking is used to overcome error. But this is not true on the spiritual level. On the spiritual level, there is but one power. Therefore, you must recognize that what is presenting itself to you is neither presence nor power: it has no law, no substance, no activity, and no reality. Therefore, no struggle with it is necessary.

"Stand still, and see the salvation of the Lord, which he will show to you today."[1] There is no battle on the spiritual level because spiritual vision recognizes that whatever the power may appear to be, it is only temporal power. Whatever the problem, no matter how big it is, it has no might. Regardless of its amount, depth, or width, it is nothing. Stand still in the realization that because God is infinite, what is appearing is nothing. It is without law, substance, or cause. There would be no errors of any nature on earth were it not for the universal belief in two powers, which acts hypnotically in your consciousness.

As a human being, you have been born into the experience of unconsciously accepting both good and evil; so it becomes necessary, if you are to come out and be separate, for you consciously to accept and demonstrate your good. You cannot wait for God to do something because God is already doing it. God already *is*.

FREEING YOURSELF FROM A UNIVERSAL MALPRACTICE

In the first half hour of waking in the morning, establish yourself in the kingdom of God. Establish yourself as living in the "secret place of the most High"[2] by bringing yourself under the law of God. Acknowledge God in praying for your enemies, learning not to malpractice, that is, learning not to see the errors that abound in the human beings about you, but rather refraining from malpractice by looking through the human appearance to the divinity that exists right there.

True protective work is the realization that God alone is power and that what appears to us—whether it is a belief of infection or contagion, a belief in hereditary disease or hereditary traits, a belief in astrology, or a belief of any other nature—exists only as universal belief. Impersonalize these beliefs. Do not blame them on any person, group of persons, race, nationality, or religion. What you personalize in any way will come back to your own doorstep because in the last analysis there is but one Self. What you ascribe to another, you are ascribing to yourself; and eventually it comes home to roost.

Miracles take place when you no longer hold persons in bondage to whatever belief is binding them. Seeing persons of ugly temperament as merely victims of universal belief tends to free them because you are not personalizing it and you are not malpracticing. Your erroneous concepts constitute a form of malpractice. Every lie you believe about another is really a form of malpractice.

Realize that all you hear on the radio, see on television, or read in the newspaper is the "arm of flesh."[3] It is without power, and you need not fear what mortal man can do because he has only temporal power, which in the face of God is no power. You have the Lord God Almighty, the All-might, the one Power. Therefore,

there is no power in all the rumors of infection, contagion, wars, and accidents. If you reject these reports of
evil in the world, when someone says, "I have the flu"
or "I have pneumonia" or "I have cancer," you will
know better than that. You will be quick to say, "Oh,
that has no power. That is not of God. Therefore, it
cannot endure."

Rather than waiting for someone to tell you of some
personal error, you could save him the experience by
spending the first half hour of the morning in the
realization that all human discord belongs to the activity
of the carnal or mortal mind, which is not a mind. It has
no law of God. It is not a power because it is not
ordained of God. Immediately impersonalize and
nothingize it.

The Nature of Protective Work

When there is the rumor of an epidemic in the air,
even though you have not heard about it, even if your
radio and television were turned off and you had
stopped the newspapers, it would manage to convey
itself to you without your conscious knowledge. Many
persons say, "This came upon me out of the blue" or "I
wasn't thinking this, and yet it happened." Evil of any
and every nature operates invisibly as a belief in two
powers; and because this is a universal belief, it acts
universally in human consciousness. To the degree you
do not consciously reject it, you become a victim of it.

It is necessary to begin every day with a form of
spiritual realization that has been called protective
work. This work is probably the most important part of
all your work in The Infinite Way. If you sufficiently

protect yourself, you will have that much less need of spiritual help to overcome anything because you will avoid those things most persons ordinarily have to overcome. Protective work is not a protection *from* anything or *from* anybody. It is protective work in the sense of protecting oneself from the operation of universal belief.

Whatever of sin, disease, lack, limitation, storms, wars, infection, or contagion may take place throughout this day is actually the operation of universal belief, carnal mind, the veil of illusion. Because this universal belief of a selfhood and a power apart from God is not God-ordained, It has no person in whom, on whom, or through whom to operate. It has no power and it has no law. As a matter of fact, it is not an "it." It is an appearance. It is an illusion. It is merely a belief that derives its seeming power by acceptance, and I hereby reject it.

I consciously reject the belief that there is any power but that of God, Spirit. I consciously reject the belief that there is a material or mental law with power because God is Spirit, and God is the only law and lawgiver. Therefore, all law must be spiritual.

Because everything that operates has to operate as law, you have nullified everything but the spiritual law of God, good, harmony, justice, equity, equality, peace, and dominion.

You have to choose when you awaken in the morning whether you are going to allow yourself to serve the universal belief in two powers or whether you are going to be God-governed. You can be God-governed only by an act of your own consciousness because without this, you, just like every other human being in the world, are subject to the powers of this world, the so-called powers of the carnal mind. You must bring yourself out from under the universal belief in two powers and establish yourself in the grace of God and realize:

There are no powers to operate in, on, or through me or anyone else except the power of God's grace.

The recognition of this truth turns hell into heaven, disease into health, sin into purity, and lack into abundance.

Your consciousness is the temple of God because God abides there. Your body is the temple of God because your consciousness is the very source, essence, and substance of your body. Your body is not something separate and apart from your consciousness. Your consciousness is formed as your body; therefore, your body is a sacred temple. It is not to be lightly spoken of or lightly dealt with. Your body is the sacred abiding place of God because God is your consciousness. God abides in you and I AM is Its name.

Nothing is more important than the first half hour of your day. In it, you establish the pattern for the day. By neglecting this, you make yourself a part of universal belief, allowing any or all of the infinite variety of universal beliefs to touch you. By faithful adherence to your realization of one Power, you separate yourself from universal belief, place yourself under the guidance of Spirit, and live out from this major principle of life.

Consciousness cannot be spiritualized to the extent of being a healing consciousness until you have sufficiently known and practiced protective work so that you begin your day steadfast in the realization of one infinite

Power. Then for the rest of the day, regardless of the appearances that touch you, you are in a position to reject them as having no power because you have established yourself in that consciousness.

You do not have to wait for the telephone to ring to bring you news of sin and disease. You do not have to wait for the radio to tell it to you. You do not have to wait for fear to descend upon you before you begin your contemplative meditation. You can prevent yourself from being overcome by these appearances, individual or worldwide, if you have established yourself in the Presence in the morning and have completely freed yourself of the belief in two powers, two laws.

The subject of law is important. Every form of evil comes in the guise of law. There is a law of economics that says there are boom times and bust times. There are economic laws of abundance and of lack, good seasons and bad seasons, upswing and downswing. There are laws behind storms, tidal waves, and all these erroneous natural phenomena.

These so-called laws are not law except as you accept them as law. The only law there can be is the law of God, and there is no other law because God is infinite. Material law—laws of matter, weather, age, infection, contagion, sin, and disease—operate only on the physical and mental levels of life. When you come to the spiritual level in which you recognize God as infinite Being, you nullify the belief that there are laws of matter or laws of mind.

All material and mental laws can be used either for good or for evil. Therefore, they cannot be of God. That which is of God can be neither good nor evil. It can only be spiritual, eternal, infinite, and perfect. There is no such thing as evil in the life and the law of God. Wherever you find the pairs of opposites, the good and the evil, you are dealing either with matter or mind. The very moment you rise above these, you find a level of consciousness in which there is not good and evil: there is only pure spiritual, infinite, eternal, harmonious being. That is life as it was in the Garden of Eden before the belief in two powers was accepted.

BECOMING A TRANSPARENCY FOR THE POWER OF SPIRIT

Whether you are practicing spiritual truth in your family circle or on a wider scale, you will not be successful if you have not formed the habit of beginning your day immersed in truth. Then, if you live and move and have your being in God-consciousness and establish yourself in the realization of one Power, none of the evils of the world will come near your dwelling place.

Your protective work is complete when you take the next step and realize that the power of good, the power of Spirit, operates from within your own being. It does not act upon you. It works out from you and acts upon this world. You are the transparency through which the law and life of God function from within you and out from you.

Just as the woman who touched the Master's robe was healed because he was a transparency through which the presence and power of God was flowing, so does your consciousness become the transparency or the instrument through which the law of God flows out into this world. It will not take six days of this practice before you notice you have changed and you feel something within. This cannot happen, however, if you think of God as separate and apart from yourself and acting on you. It comes only when you accept the Master's teaching that the kingdom of God is within you and that this presence and power of God is flowing out through and from you and acting upon this world. It acts upon the animate and the inanimate. The presence and power of God within you draws all you need in your day, operating invisibly through you out into this world.

The theme running throughout *Conscious Union with God* is: *"My oneness with God constitutes my oneness with all spiritual being and things".* As you abide in that oneness, you are one with every person in the world who belongs in your life. Every person you can bless or who can bless you is drawn into your experience. Every circumstance or thing will flow into your experience without your thinking about it. The only thought you need is the constant remembrance of your relationship to God, of the establishment of the kingdom of God within you, of the truth that all God is you are and all God has is yours.

This is your work early in the morning before your day has begun. That is why you have to awaken long before your family is up. It is not necessary to get out of bed if it is more comfortable to stay there, only do not be asleep or even half asleep when you are doing this work. It must be a conscious knowing of the truth.

As you begin your day free from the belief in two powers, established in the realization that power does not act upon you but flows out from you and that it is

---

*Joel S. Goldsmith, *Conscious Union with God*

the power of God, good, Spirit, and life, you are so established in oneness that the rest of the day, as negative appearances touch you—whether in your own experience or that of family, friends, patients, or students—you are prepared for them. When you recognize them to be only appearances without foundation or ordination, without any empowerment from God, without any law of God to support or sustain them, you will reach the depth of contemplation quickly in your healing meditation. It is then not a matter of a long routine because you have prepared your consciousness. You have spiritualized it so it instantly recognizes a negative appearance as a nothingness, an illusion, temporal power having no law of God.

THE IMPORTANCE OF SILENCE

Very few people recognize the power in silence and secrecy. As you do this work in the morning, do not speak about it to anyone. Do not even be persuaded to speak to your family about it. Keep it locked up within yourself. This is your prayer; and you want that prayer answered, not only for yourself but for all those with whom you come in contact. What you do by voicing this is ensuring it will not work. You ensure your own failure by talking about it. You are to keep these principles locked up within yourself and never discuss them except when teaching them. If a family member is receptive to spiritual work and wants to follow you on this path, it becomes your function to instruct and work with him until he becomes as adept at it as you. But voicing it at other times will ensure your loss of it.

God is your very consciousness, and this God knows the intents and the purposes of your heart. It knows your innermost nature. It is never fooled by lip service, so all the mouthing of truth you may do does not fool your consciousness. Your consciousness knows the depth and degree of your integrity.

Trying to show how much you know by telling it to others is not fooling your consciousness. It knows you are being a show-off. It knows you are trying to glorify your ego or trying to sell truth to somebody who does not want it. Your consciousness knows you do not have a noble purpose in that. You may believe you are doing good or you want to do good, but your consciousness knows that is not true. Your consciousness knows deep down in your heart you already know nobody wants truth except those who are willing to work, sacrifice, give, live, and die for it.

Work with this principle of protective work every single morning of your life, but keep it locked up within yourself and show forth by fruitage what is taking place within you. When somebody says, "How do you do it?" or "What are you doing?" do not rush to tell him. Remember you have found the "pearl of great price."[4] Let those who want it show by their sincerity, study, and devotion that they want it. And then share it. Be as liberal as you want to be with it, but first be sure. All who come saying, "Christ, Christ" do not want the Christ. The vast majority of those who come are not interested in truth. They are interested only in what they can gain from truth, in making some demonstration that is close to their heart. Help them through your secret prayers and secret knowing; but do not begin sharing it until you know the one with whom you are sharing is as devoted to it as you are, as deeply desirous of God-awareness as you are, not merely of demonstration.

God, the divine Consciousness, which is your individual consciousness, is where you are. Because It is omnipotence, It has all power to do for you. Because It is divine love, it is Its good pleasure to give you the kingdom. You need only abide in the realization of God's presence, realize God as here and now. Then you will have the mystical awareness that you can never be any place where God is not.

I in the midst of me is God. The only thing closer to me than breathing is the I *that I am. That* I, *held secretly and sacredly in my consciousness, is my bread.* I, *that I in the midst of me, has meat the world knows not of. That* I *that I am, that* I *in the midst of me, is my supply in every form: supply of companionship, supply of home, supply of health, supply of money, supply of transportation.* I *in the midst of me is the meat, the wine, and the water.*

I need never look to "man, whose breath is in his nostrils,"[5] *or seek the favor of "princes,"*[6] *because the I within me is the embodiment of my good.*

All that God is, I am. This very place I stand, heaven or hell, is holy ground.

~ 11 ~

AWAKENING TO THE SOUL-FACULTIES

WHEN we live as human beings with only our human faculties to draw upon, we present to the world and to each other a human selfhood: human qualities and human awareness. This human selfhood is always limited, always finite, consisting mostly of what we have learned through education, personal experience, environment, and prenatal influences. Hidden behind this personal self, however, is our real Self. There is another Being, another Something besides the physical and mental person. Paul called that Something the Christ, which really means the son of God, the spiritual identity of our being, the reality of us.

The sense of separation from God that arose out of what is called the Fall of Man has resulted in our limited humanhood, in which we have only our own gifts or lack of them to live by, our education or lack of it, our home experience or lack of it, and a good environment or a lack of it. These are the things that govern the human being, and yet all the time there is dormant within every person this spiritual Selfhood called the Christ, spiritual consciousness, or Christ-consciousness.

At some point in humanity's history, a stirring began within; and one here and one there found himself awakened inside through contemplation of the wonder of life. He found himself in possession of another dimension of life and saw something greater than his surroundings, greater than his own mind or brain, greater than his own wisdom. So he came into the awareness of the truth that there was dormant within him a Presence or spiritual faculty that, when awakened, enlightened him on things he could not possibly know merely through education or human knowledge.

This spiritual faculty is aroused through meditation. Inner contemplation leads to an experience in consciousness where contemplation ceases, where we no longer think—not even on spiritual things—and thought seems to settle down into a stillness, a listening attitude, a hearing attitude.

EMPTYING OUT

Attaining this silence and inner listening is not easy, but it can be done through the practice of contemplation; that is, contemplating and thinking upon some phase of spiritual Reality or some phase of truth—for example, What is God? If we knew what God is, we would be living in peace, harmony, and spiritual brotherhood. Since we do not, we scratch and fight our way through life.

We must empty ourselves of our old convictions, beliefs, and theories about God before we will ever come into an awareness of what God really is. We must be thoroughly emptied out; that is why we have periods of contemplation day after day, month after month, always finding something that God is not.

Before we come to that realization, we are so very nearly empty that we have almost convinced ourselves there is no God, and the only reason we are not wholly convinced of it is that we are alive. The very fact that we are living proves that there is life, and the very fact that there is life proves that there must be a Creator or a creative Principle. With that, we have come to the very first glimpse of what God is.

When it dawns in us that there is a great original Source and that whatever is created must be the offspring or emanation of that, we begin to look around, first, perhaps, at nature: trees, rivers, oceans, or mountains. We become aware that the world of nature is governed by law. There are actual laws, such as those that bring the tides up so far and no further; those that make the tides recede so far and no further. Through contemplation, we become aware that the stars, the sun, and the moon are always in orbit, always under some divine order or law. As we continue, we realize all that is taking place in the nature of creation or unfoldment and governed by law is taking place without any person praying for it, without any person telling God what to do about it or when to do it. One season follows another in regular order, and no one is telling God what to do about it.

FINDING OUR PLACE IN THE SCHEME OF LIFE

With more and more contemplation, we begin to perceive the very nature of God and see how wrong we have been in trying to influence Him or in trying to move Him to do our will. Eventually, through contemplation, we find our place in the scheme of life.

Did God send me into expression and then turn me loose? Or is God still with me and have I been ignoring Him? Is it possible that the God that sent me into manifestation is still here governing me as God is governing the tides, the sun, the moon, and the stars? Is it possible there is a God leading me, guiding me, directing me and I have closed my eyes and ears to Him and locked myself up within myself and thought I could be a go-getter and do it all?

There is a God; there is that which sent me into manifestation and expression, that which caused me to be born. Did God not tell me He was with me "before Abraham was," [1] *He would be with me unto the end of the world, and He would never leave me or forsake me?*

Gradually, we begin to understand that the sages of old, the spiritual seers, knew this Presence was within them and within everyone and It would never leave them. They could relax in It, rest in It, let It pick them up, let It guide them, let It direct them. So, through this contemplation, wisdom is being revealed to us from a Source within ourselves we could not and did not receive through education.

Thus, we are led back through questions to answers. We are doing the questioning, but the answers are coming from a Source within that is not human, from Something greater than ourselves. We ask the questions in our ignorance, and the answers reveal themselves to us from within. Only we must be bold; we must not fear to ask questions, pertinent and even impertinent questions. Let us not fear to say, "I wonder if there is a God," and begin with that premise and then go back and see where it leads us. Or we may begin with, "Well, I must assume there is a God from all I have seen of the world. So I will begin with the assumption that there is a God and that I do not know what God is, but neither does anybody else I know about," and see if we cannot find a solution.

Abraham, Isaac, Jacob, Moses, Elijah, Jesus, John, Paul, Buddha, and Lao-Tse all had close relationships with God. We can, too. True, they made themselves more important to this world by the vision and the wisdom they have given us. They are more important to this world than a thousand of us, but they are not more important to God than any one of us.

In the eyes of God, the child of God is our true identity; we are offspring of God. "And call no man your father upon the earth: for one is your Father, which is in heaven."[2] That means your Father and my Father, and Jesus' Father, John's Father, Lao-Tse's Father, and Buddha's Father. There is but one Father, one Source of life, one Life stream. It is pouring Itself forth as our individual identity, and we have never lost that individual identity. All that happens is we become wiser, more spiritual in expression, and more meaningful to the world in proportion to our recognition that the Source of being is within ourselves.

This contemplation, which begins as a purely human or mental activity, gradually leads us back step by step to a place within our own consciousness where the answer pops out at us, the right answer, the answer that has always been available, if only we had stopped taking somebody else's word for it. If we must have someone's authority for it, let us take only the word of those who have endured through the centuries as recognized spiritual lights. They all agree the kingdom of God is within us, and they all agree the name of God is *I:*

"I AM THAT I AM." [3] I *in the midst of thee am mighty. It is* I *that was with thee in the beginning. The substance of*

Life–the Essence, the Life stream, the Source, the creative Principle–is I.

All this begins to unfold within through questioning ourselves, contemplating, being willing to empty ourselves of preconceived beliefs, and opening ourselves to an inner wisdom in the assurance that "My grace is sufficient for thee."[4] The grace of God will give us the answer to every problem if we remember that the grace of God is within us.

If we recognize the place we stand is holy ground, then we can turn to the Father within any time of the day or night. If we do not receive our answer immediately, let us remember how many centuries we have been unaware of our Source. Now we are awakening that inner faculty, bringing that Father within to conscious realization, bringing to light the manna that has been hidden in us.

AWAKENING THE SOUL-CENTER

The contemplative form of meditation awakens us to the Christ, that spiritual Center, that Soul-faculty; and then a whole new experience opens to us. We are never again alone; we are never again living our own life by our own power exclusively. After we have been awakened to this dormant faculty, we are open to a Presence within us. Sometimes we are actually conscious of it as a Presence; but even when we are not, we know it is there by the way our life is being lived, by the fruitage. It is a Presence that goes before us to arrange things for us, do for us, and prepare for us, to prepare those "many mansions."[5] Perhaps some phase of our business that was being blocked is suddenly opened; some idea that has been hidden from us all of a sudden comes into manifestation and expression; or some inner guidance comes.

A miracle happens in our experience when we begin to know that God is the mind of man. If God is the mind of man, we are all in that one mind and have that one mind. We are one, and our interests are one. If God is our mind, all that is known to God is known to every one of us equally. Because God is our mind, if we know our own integrity, so does everybody else who can ever be brought into our sphere. That is why we are told to be still. We do not have to go out and shout because whatever is known in silence and secrecy, God reveals openly. This is Grace, but that Grace cannot touch us until we have become consciously aware that God is the mind of all mankind.

If anything can play an important part in our life—a book, a teaching, a teacher, or a talent—by our knowing that God is the mind of man, we draw it unto us. It may be on the other side of the world; but instantly it will be started on its way to us. One of these days we will wake up and find we have the very thing that was so necessary to us and humanly we did nothing about, except to know the truth of God as the mind of all mankind. Knowing the truth frees us from the sense of limitation. As we abide in the truth that God is the mind, the life, and the love of man, we let our good and our love come to us through anyone and everyone.

This spiritual Wisdom operates in the most mundane of our affairs, even as to what investments to buy and sell and when. This is not because God has any knowledge of whether the stock market is going up or down but because an inner faculty of discernment, which we are able to utilize in connection with any and every form of activity, is aroused in us.

We are concerned not that God knows what we should buy or sell, for whom we should work, or what line of merchandise we should represent but that we have awakened to this Soul-faculty. It knows exactly what we are to do and directs us to it, even if it is something that ordinarily would not have come to our attention. Therefore, we are not concerned now with what is out here but with the attainment of this awakened sense of the Christ-faculty.

THE SPIRIT DRIVES US TO ITSELF

The first step in this awakening is a step we did not take; it was taken for us. Something pointed us in the direction of a spiritual teaching, and that was the very first factor in our awakening. That should be proof there is Something greater than ourselves operating in our inner parts; there is Something operating in our consciousness guiding us, supplying and sustaining us, Something operating in our consciousness of which we may not have been aware.

Being sold into slavery took Joseph away from his family and home to become the second in command of a nation. It brought Joseph into Egypt and made it possible for him to be second to the ruler and become the great mind of Egypt. Without that, he would have remained at home, the pampered son of a rich man; and he probably would have amounted to very little. Many of us have come to whatever state of realization we have only because some sickness, sin, unhappiness, or failure compelled us to find this hidden manna, this *I* that is our meat, our wine, our water, this *I* that is within us that is mighty, this *I* that goes before us.

The Soul that is God is the Soul of man, and this Soul of man has a function to perform in our experience. The Soul is really the Source of man's light, good, capacities, and integrity. When we rely on our Soul rather than on an externalized form of matter or person, we are fulfilling the original intent of Scripture and of prayer. True prayer is meant to destroy our faith in anything and everything that can be seen, heard, tasted, touched, or smelled. It removes our faith from effect.

Whatever we have placed faith in or on can and in many cases does break down. It leaves us without hope, reliance, or substance in our experience. Very often we are driven to God by such experiences; and when we are driven to God, we are really driven to a reliance on that invisible part of us that is the Soul.

As we learn to withdraw our gaze from the external realm and turn it to the Soul of man within us, we begin to bring the glories of God into our experience. We can retire from the world into the temple of our being, meaning we can retire into our Soul, which is at our center.

There is only one Soul; and this is my Soul and the Soul of every person. It is with us individually and collectively as a source of light, grace, and peace. The Soul is my reliance. The Soul is my hiding place and my abiding place; the Soul is the temple of God. The Soul is the source of the living waters. The Soul has within It the capacity for my resurrection, redemption, and regeneration.

This Soul is incorporeal, spiritual, infinite, and therefore omnipresent. It is right here where we are, but It requires the stillness of the mind for us to make contact with It. It is from the Soul that the Voice comes and says, "*My* Grace is thy sufficiency; *My* life is thy life; *My* peace is thy peace." It is from the Soul that safety and security flow. The Soul is the source of life eternal, life harmonious, and life joyous. In the Soul are all the issues of life, the opportunities for service and for fruitage of all kinds.

None of the terrors by night or by day, none of the snares, none of the pitfalls comes near the dwelling place of those who dwell in their Soul, who live, move, and have their being in their Soul, whose reliance, confidence, and hope are in the Soul, who look to their Soul always for nourishment, Grace, peace, resurrection, and regeneration.

When we know and recognize our Soul as the Source of our life, our continuity and fruitage, we live our outer life normally and joyously, watching its coming and going without fear and without discouragement because of the renewal that immediately begins to take place within the Soul. In our Soul we find our rest and refreshment.

When we open our consciousness that it may be filled with the Spirit of God, with no reason, no object, no purpose, just that consciousness may be filled with that Spirit, It ordains us. Some are ordained to heal the sick; some are ordained to minister in other ways to the sick; some are ordained to work in art, literature, or music. Wherever the Spirit of God touches the consciousness of an individual, he is ordained and made fruitful in an activity or given some new activity.

OPENING THE WAY FOR GOD'S PURPOSE
TO BE REVEALED

The spiritual life has its foundation in the realization that "I and my Father are one."[6] Therefore, all that God is, is ours. We rest in the realization that we are already fulfilled so we now have no right to desire any particular work, even of a spiritual nature, because that would be acknowledging a lack.

Our attitude in the spiritual life is always one of living, moving, and having our being in God-awareness, opening ourselves to spiritual realization and unfoldment, listening for the "still small voice."[7] That is all. Then, when we are up in the morning, whatever is given us to do, that we must do. If one is in business or some profession, one must go out and tend to that work. If one keeps house, one must see to the obligations of the home. There must be no further desire than to do what is at hand, to do it to the highest of our understanding and with the advantage of receiving God's grace.

In performing our activity in that way and with no further desires, hopes, or ambitions, we constantly illuminate and enrich consciousness. The day will come, then, when some spiritual activity is demanded of us. It is possible that, as we continue our spiritual unfoldment, study, and meditation, we may be led into some activity the world calls spiritual. But this will not necessarily occur. Many persons are made more useful in their present activity than they could possibly be if they were moved into some other. Some develop, through their spiritual study and preparation, in a way they had not imagined possible. If everyone became a practitioner or a spiritual teacher, it would leave all our bridges unbuilt and all the other necessary work of the world undone. No one should ever desire to be a practitioner or a teacher, because it is really a wrong desire.

Elijah and Elisha were talking about this very thing one day. Elijah asked Elisha what he could do for him before he was taken away. Elisha said, "I pray thee, let a double portion of thy spirit be upon me."[8] When Elijah "went up by a whirlwind into heaven,"[9] Elisha was able to take "the mantle of Elijah that fell from him,"[10] because he had witnessed Elijah's ascension. If a person has the spiritual perception to witness the ascension, he has spiritual discernment, which will be his robe or spiritual consciousness to carry him forward.

LETTING GOD'S PURPOSE BE REVEALED IN US

Meditation is opening one's self to God's grace, direction, and guidance. It is putting our personal selfhood aside and acknowledging God in everything we do. It is not leaning unto our own understanding and asking God to bless what we want. It is really showing forth God's will, God's way, and God's glory. We have asked nothing for ourselves. We open the way for Grace to take over by laying down our will, plan, hopes, and ambitions—even when they are good and noble. These must be put aside in order for us to become transparencies for God, and this can be accomplished only through prayer and meditation.

Many of us must have asked ourselves why we are on earth, why we were born, why we continue to take up space on this earth, what our purpose is, and what function we perform in being here. If we try to answer these questions from any human standpoint, we will be wrong. We are not here to be a wife, husband, mother, or father. We are not here to be successful in business, art, or a profession. We are not here to accomplish good on earth. We are here only for one purpose, and that is to fulfill God's purpose in us—not our purpose. Regardless of how good or how noble our purpose might be, if it is *our* purpose, we are wrong. Instead, let us put ourselves aside and realize:

God created me, and God created me for His purpose, not mine. God created me to perform His will on earth, not for me to decide what I want to be, what I want to do, or where I want to do it. That would be having a mind and a will apart from God. Let not my will be done, but "Thy will be done in earth, as it is in heaven."[11]

The kingdom of God can never come on earth for me as long as I am attempting to fulfill my own will, my own desire, because I am blocking God out of my life.

Let me know Thy will, and I will follow it. Make Thy will evident in me. Lead me in the way that Thou wishest me to go. Let me on earth be a fulfillment of Thy plan. Let me on earth be the showing forth of Thy glory so that wherever I go it will be said there is the presence of God. Let no attention be called to my personal accomplishments.

God feels and senses our motive. Very often our words make liars of our motives or our motives make liars of our words. We are praying for one thing with the lips and the mind, and the heart is really turned in another direction. But we are not fooling God; we are fooling ourselves. There has to be a purity of motive, and part of that purity is in the surrender of any personal will.

Let Thy will be done in me. Let me know Thy will. Unmistakably, let me know Thy will, and I will follow it. Let me know Thy way, the way I am to go.

~ 12 ~

CONSCIOUSNESS UNFOLDING
AS THE HARMONY
OF OUR EXPERIENCE

SOME time ago a poll was conducted across the United States on the question of what would contribute the most to peace. Thirty-eight percent of those interviewed felt uniting under one God would do more to ensure peace than a greater stockpile of bombs, more armaments, or disarmament. This indicates the beginning of a change of consciousness, and it is on this that valid prophecies can be made. With thirty-eight percent of a cross section of the population agreeing that spiritual values will do more for peace than atomic bombs, we can be assured that a change of consciousness, which will ensure ultimate peace, is evolving.

Nearly every war that has not grown out of business rivalry has resulted from religious differences. Among religious groups, there are those who claim the Hebrews are God's chosen people, the Catholics have the only one true God, and the Protestants have the right way. Always there is the belief there is a God for each religion and this is the one and only God. But when thirty-eight percent of the persons interviewed agree there is only one God, bias, bigotry, and religious differences are being wiped out. The important thing is the recognition that whether we are Occidental or Oriental, white or black, Jew or Gentile, we are worshiping the same God. Then we have universality.

Understanding there is but one God changes the nature of the individual. It changes the nature of our relationship with others because the greatest difference has been removed: believing there is one God for you and another God for me.

At the beginning of every year, all kinds of predictions are made: predictions as to whether business will go forward or backward, as to the possibilities of peace, as to how the government will function. There are those, of course, who attempt to guess or make predictions based on astrological charts. As a rule, some of these come to pass, perhaps ten, twelve, or fifteen percent of the time, even though very few of these predictions are based on anything that would give them validity.

A prediction, in order to be relied upon, must be based on a change of consciousness. If there is no change of consciousness, there can be no change in outer conditions. If, on entering a new year, our consciousness is the same consciousness with which we came into the previous year, we can be sure of duplicating the previous year's experience. But if our consciousness has deepened and been enriched, the new year will be enriched.

Nothing happens except as a projection of consciousness. Neither time nor space has any action in it. The action is projected by consciousness, individually and collectively. We are affected by our consciousness, which brings back to us the experiences that take place.

For example, what happens if I accept the metaphysical and mystical revelation of God as individual consciousness, God constituting my consciousness, which is equivalent to the Master's statement, "The kingdom of God is within you"?[1] Immediately, I begin to lose faith, reliance, or dependence on anyone or anything external to me. I have begun to realize that whatever power is to be exercised in and for the benefit of my life must flow from within me.

My gaze is now taken away from the world and centered on the kingdom of God, the power, the love, and the Grace within me. At the same time, my fear of the external world—germs, wrong thinking, and outside powers of any kind—is lessened. Even in the midst of a war, I would feel safe because the kingdom of God, the kingdom of real power, is within me. Though a thousand should fall at my left and ten thousand at my right, I know harm could not come near my dwelling place because I am resting in the realization of God—Omnipresence, Omnipotence, Omniscience—here where I am. In war or peace, sickness or health, regardless of outer circumstances, I would be anchored in the presence and power of God constituting my very being.

Established in this consciousness, I could prophecy that my new year would have less in it of disagreements with my neighbor, less of sin or false appetite, and less of disease because in this consciousness of God's presence and power, evil cannot operate. Therefore, my state of consciousness would determine the nature of my year—not one hundred percent because I have not yet attained one hundred percent of God awareness, but to the extent I have attained any measure of God awareness, it would operate for harmony and peace in my individual life.

BECOMING A SOCIETY OF FRIENDS AND NEIGHBORS

In the relationship of all those who have accepted one God, omnipresent, omniscient, and omnipotent, there would be peace; there would be harmony; there would be a loving of their neighbor as themselves. Whatever of discord and inharmony comes into their experience would still be a universal belief they had not completely overcome.

I can predict good for myself only to the extent my consciousness is enriched and deepened in its realization of God, omnipresent, omniscient, and omnipotent. What I give out will come back to me. The bread I cast on the water will return to me. Therefore, as I individually realize God constitutes the consciousness of mankind, friend and enemy, Jew and Gentile, white and black, Oriental and Occidental, in the degree I can see oneness of consciousness, I am loving my neighbor as myself. I am recognizing that all God is to me, God is to my neighbor; and I am therefore giving out love, truth, and neighborliness. In a measure, this is what will come back to me.

Because of the years of ignorance of this truth, it is necessary to renew day by day this consciousness of God as constituting the life and being of mankind. As we begin to adopt this as our way of life, we become a society of friends and neighbors, a society of God-conscious, God-loving people. When as many as thirty-eight percent of a cross section of the population agree there is one God, it must be obvious this consciousness is spreading. It is safe to predict we are coming closer to a permanent peace on earth because we are coming closer to a united consciousness of one God.

Over the past ten years, there has been an ever-widening interest in the subject of spiritual healing. This is another example of a oneness of consciousness coming into being. It makes little difference whether spiritual healing is thought of from the standpoint of one particular teaching or another. The important point is that consciousness is becoming united on the truth of God as Power in human existence.

Until this century, God has been presented principally as a power in the world hereafter. There is a feeling that what good God does not give a person here will undoubtedly be given one in the next world. But bringing God specifically into our day-to-day health, supply, neighborly relationships, or international relationships has come about fairly recently. This is another evidence of a uniting of consciousness and an agreement there is God on earth as there is God in heaven.

The more we recognize there is no such thing as a Baptist God, an Episcopalian God, a Presbyterian God, a metaphysical God, or an orthodox God but that there is only one God, the closer we come to a united consciousness and the more God-consciousness is loosed on earth.

The Master's ministry was not merely one of healing the sick. It was equally devoted to forgiving the sinner, not after centuries of punishment in hell or in some anteroom of hell and not after centuries of suffering under karmic law, but in the very moment of his looking up. The entire ministry of the Christ was to show that in the moment of turning, in the recognition of the Christ, of spiritual Grace, we are saved. This is the most difficult part of attaining the new consciousness because it has been ingrained in us that we must suffer for our sins. This is part of the error that exists in our legal world today, an error that can be overcome only by the spiritualization of consciousness. Persons are put in prison as a punishment for offenses and then released to commit the same crimes again without any regard as to whether or not there has been a change of consciousness. It is very evident that a person released from prison in the same consciousness in which he went in is the same person and is likely to commit the same crimes again.

Someday prisoners will not be released until they have demonstrated a change of consciousness. Then it will be safe to release them. There is no guesswork as to how many crimes a criminal is going to commit. He is going to commit crimes over and over again until his consciousness has been changed. When his consciousness has been changed, he will commit no more crimes.

Our state of consciousness determines our experience, and those who have attained the consciousness of one God are right now laying the foundation for the peace of the future.

THE MYSTICAL CONSCIOUSNESS OF ONENESS, THE SECRET OF BROTHERHOOD

As you and I individually, without regard for any family member, friend, or neighbor, concern ourselves with attaining God-consciousness, even if we attain It only in a measure, we are determining the harmony of our experience. Then, as our own consciousness deepens and ripens, our consciousness begins to become a law unto our relatives, friends, and neighbors. We begin to draw them into this same consciousness and eventually discover what was originally our God-consciousness has now become the God-consciousness of many.

One individual—whether a metaphysical practitioner, a minister, a rabbi, or a priest—becomes a law unto all those drawn into the orbit of his consciousness, at first in a very minor degree but gradually in a larger degree, until suddenly there is a community of God-consciousness.

Once we can acknowledge one God, we will acknowledge one truth; then there can be no differences that divide us. We will be what the Master revealed we are: brothers. We all have one Father, *the* Father. Group differences disappear in the consciousness of that one God, one Truth.

The world is looking for peace on earth, and I have no doubt it eventually is going to get it. But neither have I any hesitancy in prophesying it is not going to happen until the truth-students, the Protestants, and the Catholics can unite in praying for one another. We cannot have peace on earth while Christian sects cannot pray for or agree with each other. We talk Christianity; we talk Christ; we talk truth; and we talk love. Then we manifest jealousy, envy, and rivalry toward one another.

The mystical way of life knows no such thing as a denomination. The Spirit of the Lord God either is upon us or It is not. If It is, It is whether we are a Catholic, a Protestant, a Jew, or a Moslem.

I have a friend in Cairo, Egypt, who is a very devout Moslem. One time he sent me a set of beautiful amber beads that had been blessed in Mecca. Greater love hath no Moslem than to part with beads that have received that holy blessing. I had his business address, but not his home address. I arrived in Cairo at three o'clock one Sunday morning. On one of those perfect days for which Cairo is famous, I was up at eight o'clock. Not knowing my friend's home address, I could not find him. With nothing to do all day, I walked aimlessly about and was led to a big circle from which streets radiated in all directions. I walked past one and turned down another, and there was my friend standing up against a building with a set of beads in his hands praying. I walked over to him. "Abdul!" "Goldsmith! I'm praying for you." "What do you mean, you're praying for me?" "I told my wife this morning I can't wait any longer. You must come. I need you; so I'm going out somewhere and just pray that you come to Cairo." I had come right to the place where he was praying, and I have a feeling that my desire to be led wherever God would lead me—The Infinite Way desire—was matched by his Moslem prayer.

That is the nature of the oneness of the mystical consciousness. Mysticism is conscious union with God, the ability to receive impartations directly from God. It does not mention anything about demonstration, race, religion, color, clime, or creed. But we cannot fulfill the mission and the message of the Master to bring life and bring it more abundantly or to bring healing, supply, or spiritual illumination to anyone unless we ourselves have that Christ. *It* heals. *It* redeems. *It* saves. *It* raises from the dead. *It* feeds.

The mission of the Christ must be understood first by us and then by our example shown to others so the world will ask, "How is this accomplished? Even the most religious of men and women have not been able to do these works." And our answer will be, "When the

Spirit of the Lord God is upon us, we can do these works through that Spirit because then that Spirit does these works through us."

ORDINATION BY THE SPIRIT

Too many have brought to their work only the intellectual knowledge of what they have read in books. All they know is statements of truth. They have not yet prepared themselves to receive ordination, to receive the Spirit of God within them. Reading it in a book will not do it. Loving it and having zeal will not do it. Wanting to save the world will not do it. One thing alone will do it: go away and study; be secret; be sacred; let no one know what you are doing. Study until the finger of God touches you and you find yourself ordained. Then you will not have to go out to find your work. Then the world will beat a path to your door. That is the better mousetrap you can have, that Spirit of the Lord God.

You will feel this Something within you closer than breathing, Something sitting on your shoulder, walking just behind you, or standing there. You will recognize this Presence, and you will know Its power—feel It, and even hear the "still small voice."[2] Then you can say,

"The Spirit of the Lord God is upon me." [3] *Now I am ordained: not through my intellect, my wisdom, my strength, my knowledge, or my zeal. Now I am a soldier under orders. I have the armor of the Spirit of the Lord upon me—which is the word of God—not the words in a book, but the word of God, which is life and love.*

Then you can walk into the home of the sick, the poor, the dying, or the dead and bring consolation, healing, resurrection, supply, all things.

Never be guilty of believing pain or any circumstance is an obstacle to the search for God. When you have attained the awareness of God, the pain, the discord, and the disease will leave. The poorer you are and the greater your need, the greater is your need for God. Seek God first, and you will find yourself free. If you try to get your freedom first, you never will get God.

There are those who will not give up an hour or two of sleep. There are those who will not take ten minutes out of every hour for study and meditation. But that does not for a moment mean there is anyone in this world seriously intent on the spiritual experience who cannot have it. True, he cannot have all of it in a day; he cannot have all of it in five or even ten years. It takes devotion, consecration, and seriousness. The goal is not name or fame because even if you had it, you would be too busy to make much use of it. The goal is the attainment of this Spirit of the Lord God, the attainment of this awareness. That is the entire goal of the spiritual life.

What It does with you after you attain It is Its business. Whatever you do with the Spirit of the Lord working in you, you do well. Whatever you do when the Spirit of the Lord God is upon you, you do better than anyone else could do without that Spirit. You cannot know what your field of activity is to be; you cannot have an ambition to be any particular thing. If you do, you must be prepared to change at any moment because you can have no idea what the Spirit of the Lord God will do to you when It descends upon you.

There is but one demonstration for those who wish to be disciples: demonstrate the Presence; have the feeling of this Presence within you, about you, or next to you. Then when you have It, you "take no thought for your life, what ye shall eat; neither for the body, what ye shall put on."[4] You take no thought for your life whatsoever—not for anything. The Spirit functions and becomes your daily bread; It functions and becomes your business opportunity; It becomes your talent, ability, skill, and bodily strength. There is only It, and that It is your demonstration. That is your goal.

This Christ, which is the Essence or Substance of all form, demonstrates Itself as everything necessary in your experience. This is mysticism. It is Self-completeness in God. The Christ of God, the Spirit of God is within; and the Holy Ghost is the bond between the Father and the Son.

The mystical life is a life built on the Spirit of God. The life of the aspirant is devoted to study, meditation, and communion with those who have gone beyond him on this path and through whom he can receive illumination until the Spirit of the Lord God enters him and he finds himself ordained. From then on, each is on his own.

With this for a foundation, we are building the consciousness that will enable us to live twenty-four hours each day and seven days a week in the awareness of Divinity: divine Power, divine Grace within our very own being. This will ultimately set the world free. It is not a teaching, a religion, or a teacher that is going to set the world free. If any teacher could have set the world free, Buddha or Jesus Christ would have done it long ago. Neither one has set the world free, and no teacher ever will.

Only one thing will set the world free: the consciousness of divine Grace within you and me and all mankind. As we begin to see proofs of this in our experience
and have experiences that show us that Grace is operating, we will look out at everyone in our community with
the attitude, "Isn't this wonderful? I can set you free by
realizing the kingdom of Grace is operating within you.
It will not let evil come near your dwelling place. It will
not let sin, false appetite, disease, or man's inhumanity
to man come near you."

Instead of feeling responsible for people in the sense
of becoming do-gooders, we look out at this world with
a smile and a "Thank You, Father, for having revealed
to me that the kingdom of Grace is operating in the
consciousness of every individual." As each one becomes aware of the kingdom of Grace operating within
him, a year of fulfillment is assured. Nothing else can
assure it.

Peace on earth will never come through armaments
or wars; peace on earth will never come through
agreements between nations because there have been
agreements between nations since long "before Abraham was."[5] None of them has ever been honored any
longer than it served the purpose of the nation that
signed it. Any and every nation has broken the agreements it signed when it suited its purpose. Therefore,
peace will never come by agreement. Peace will come
when there is peace in people's hearts. There is only
one thing that will bring that peace: the realization of
divine Grace within.

Gratitude will not bring it. No nation is going to be
grateful for the help another nation has given it. Nations
never have and never will be grateful, just as very

seldom is there a real sense of gratitude in those we help humanly, certainly not one lasting very long. One thing alone brings peace: the realization of a divine Grace operating within the consciousness of each and every one of us. As fully as we realize this Grace within us, It brings peace to us. As we begin to perceive this Grace operating in the consciousness of mankind, in that degree will this Christ-Spirit be awakened in mankind.

GRACE FUNCTIONING AS LOVE

It is not a matter of the intellect; it is a matter of perception. No one can understand divine Grace with the mind because no one can see sufficient evidence of it with the mind. Grace is an activity of God that we become aware of through an inner perception. It is Grace that frees the sinner, that frees those in lack and limitation, and that frees those in disease. There is no other power than this divine Grace functioning within us, and Its mode of functioning is through love. Then we are permitting love, not our love, but God's love, to flow through us in the form of forgiving "seventy times seven,"[6] in the form of praying for our enemies and for those who persecute us.

Love is exemplified in visiting the sick. We visit the sick, not always by going to their household and sitting there, holding hands, and pitying them, but through our awakened consciousness, realizing the divine Grace that sets them free. We visit those in prison, sometimes physically, but always spiritually. Because of the incorporeal nature of our being, we do not always have to do the things physically that people of the world seem to find necessary. Knowing themselves only as physical beings, they can visit those in prison or those who are sick only by visiting them personally. Having realized the nature of Grace, however, we can visit the sinner, the sick, or the prisoner and set them free without ever leaving our home. The incorporeal or spiritual nature of our being makes it possible for us to be present in spirit with the sick, the sinning, and the imprisoned. And it is the Spirit that makes them free, not our physical body.

Carrying our physical body to the sick or to the prisoner does not make them free. It is what is embodied in our consciousness that sets them free; that is why the actual physical visiting is at a minimum. The spiritual visiting is a twenty-four-hour-a-day occupation.

Consciousness determines the nature of our experience and our year: what we have in consciousness, what we know in consciousness, what we are holding in consciousness, what we are loosing in consciousness. The truth we know becomes a law unto our experience. The truth we know becomes a law unto our neighbor. All this knowing of the truth is a deepening and enriching of our individual consciousness.

As our consciousness is enriched, the world, too, is enriched because "I, if I be lifted Up"[7] am drawing up, in some measure, the entire world. I, as an individual, may lift it up only a millimeter; but when we are a hundred individuals, we are lifting it up a hundred millimeters. When there are a thousand individuals, we are lifting it up immeasurably and probably even multiplying that by the fact of our unity and oneness of consciousness.

As long as we can be made to believe that anyone in this world can give or take from us, in that degree we are either dependent upon him or fear him. The moment we realize divine Grace alone feeds us, heals us, supplies us, and forgives us we attain our freedom in Christ. Divine Grace assures us we have meat the world knows not of. Divine Grace assures us of our bread. We need take no thought for our life as we walk on this earth. If necessary, we can walk in poverty for a while or in sin or in disease. But always while we are in this sin, disease, or poverty there is the son of God, the divine Grace within us. One day It will break loose.

Abide in this Word; abide in It; live in It: "I have meat to eat that ye know not of."[8] This is the Christ message; we have meat, wine, water, and resurrection. We have within us a Presence planted there by God that we might have life and we might have it more abundantly. If we live in this awareness morning to night and night to morning, the crust of human demonstration will break and the spiritual demonstration will come through. Only in this way can we be assured of a permanent and glorious experience.

Notes

Scriptural references are from the King James Version

1. The Atheism of Material Power

1. II Samuel 22:2.
2. Acts 17:28.
3. Acts 5:18,19.
4. John 17:15.
5. John 16:33.
6. John 15:13.
7. John 17:20.
8. I Corinthians 13:3.
9. Matthew 5:28.
10. I Corinthians 15:31.
11. John 1:14.
12. Psalm 138:8.
13. I John 4:4.
14. Ephesians 5:14.
15. Revelation 21:27.
16. Zechariah 4:6.
17. II Chronicles 20:17.
18. II Chronicles 32:8.
19. I Kings 19:12.
20. Luke 8:46.

2. Releasing Spiritual Power

1. Mark 2:9.
2. Matthew 21:12.
3. Matthew 5:39.
4. Matthew 26:52.
5. II Corinthians 3:17.
6. Psalm 16:11.
7. John 4:32.
8. Matthew 14:27.
9. Zechariah 4:6.
10. John 18:36.
11. I Corinthians 2:14.
12. Romans 8:7.
13. Romans 8:20.
14. Galatians 2:20.
15. Luke 15:31.
16. Romans 8:38, 39.
17. John 12:32.
18. Matthew 7:1.
19. Luke 23:34.
20. Matthew 18:22.

3. Spiritual Power Unveiled

1. John 19:10, 11.
2. John 14:27.
3. John 18:36.
4. Isaiah 2:4
5. Mark 4:39.
6. Ezekiel 18:32.
7. John 6:38.
8. John 8:58.
9. Matthew 28:20.
10. Matthew 5:39.
11. Matthew 26:52.
12. Isaiah 31:5.
13. Psalm 139:8.
14. Psalm 23.4.
15. Isaiah 2:22.
16. Isaiah 33:20, 24.
17. John 18:36.
18. Matthew 26:52.
19. John 16:33.
20. Galatians 2:20.
21. Philippians 4:13.
22. I Kings 19:12.
23. Exodus 13:21.
24. Exodus 16:15.
25. Philippians 4:7.

4. Flesh and Flesh

1. Isaiah 40:6.
2. John 6:63.
3. John 1:14.
4. John 9:25.
5. Job 19:26.
6. John 5:30.
7. Acts 17:28.
8. I Kings 19:12.
9. Psalm 146:3.
10. II Corinthians 5:16.
11. II Corinthians 5:17.
12. II Corinthians 5:1, 2, 4.

5. Our Real Identity

1. I Samuel 2:9.
2. Psalm 23:4.
3. Isaiah 2:22.
4. Psalm 118:9.
5. John 8:58.
6. Romans 7:19.
7. Philippians 3:13.
8. Matthew 18:22.
9. John 16:33.
10. Isaiah 55:8.
11. Matthew 6:13.
12. Revelation 3:20.
13. John 4:32.
14. Isaiah 45:2.
15. Zechariah 4:6.
16. Exodus 14:13.
17. Galatians 2:20.

6. The Word and Words

1. I Kings 19:12.
2. John 5:31.
3. Job 23:14.

4. Isaiah 62:12.
5. John 14:27.
6. Hebrews 4:12.

7. Concepts or Is?

1. John 19:11
2. Matthew 19:17.

3. John 7:24.
4. Matthew 3:17.

8. Attaining Dominion Through *I*

1. John 10:30.
2. John 8:58.
3. Matthew 9:6.
4. Exodus 3:14.
5. John 12:32.

6. Isaiah 2:22.
7. Matthew 7:12.
8. Isaiah 40:4.
9. John 14:2.

9. The Mystic and Healing

1. Isaiah 2:22.
2. Galatians 2:20.
3. Philippians 4:13.
4. John 19:11.
5. Isaiah 61:1.
6. John 8:32.
7. John 8:11.
8. John 6:35.

9. Exodus 3:14.
10. John 10:30.
11. Psalm 23:4.
12. John 8:46.
13. Isaiah 42:8.
14. Psalm 23:1.
15. Psalm 23:2.
16. John 8:58.

10. Dominion Through Daily Realization

1. Exodus 14:13.
2. Psalm 91:1.
3. II Chronicles 32:8.

4. Matthew 13:46.
5. Isaiah 2:22.
6. Psalm 146:3.

11. AWAKENING TO THE SOUL-FACULTIES

1. John 8:58.
2. Matthew 23:9.
3. Exodus 3:14.
4. II Corinthians 12:9.
5. John 14:2.
6. John 10:30.
7. I Kings 19:12.
8. II Kings 2:9.
9. II Kings 2:11.
10. II Kings 2:14.
11. Matthew 6:10.

12. CONSCIOUSNESS UNFOLDING AS THE HARMONY OF OUR EXPERIENCE

1. Luke 17:21.
2. I Kings 19:12.
3. Isaiah 61:1.
4. Luke 12:22.
5. John 8:58.
6. Matthew 18:22.
7. John 12:32.
8. John 4:32.

Tape Recordings

The following tape recordings of classes and talks given by Joel S. Goldsmith were used in the preparation of this book:

1. The Atheism of Material Power

    1. "Cease Ye from Man Whose Breath Is in His Nostrils," *The 1958 Second Sydney and Melbourne Closed Class*, Reel 1, Side 1.
    2. "Antidote for Fear," *The 1958 Second Sydney and Melbourne Closed Class*, Reel 1, Side 2.

2. Releasing Spiritual Power

    1. "Spiritual Power, Temporal Nonpower," *The 1962 London Special Class*, Reel 1, Side 1.
    2. "The Nature of Spiritual Power," *The 1962 London Special Class*, Reel 1, Side 2.

3. Spiritual Power Unveiled

    1. "Spiritual Power Unveiled," *The 1961 Canadian Special Class*, Reel 1, Side 2.
    2. "Mystically Living by the Hearing of the Word of God," *The 1962 Mission Inn Closed Class*, Reel 1, Side 2.
    3. "The Messiah," *The 1962 Mission Inn Closed Class*, Reel 3, Side 2.

4. Flesh and Flesh

1. "Flesh and Flesh," *The 1954 First Portland Practitioners' Class*, Reel 1, Side 2; Reel 2, Side 1.
2. "Infinite Way Principles," *The 1954 First Portland Practitioners' Class*, Reel 1, Side 1.

5. Our Real Identity

1. "Our Real Identity and Oneness," *The 1954 Portland Practitioners' Class*, Reel 4, Side 1.
2. "The Word Made Flesh," *The 1962 Hamburg, Germany, Closed Class*, Reel 2, Side 2.

6. The Word and Words

1. "Flesh and Flesh," *The 1954 First Portland Practitioners' Class*, Reel 2, Side 1; Reel 1, Side 2
2. "Law and Grace," *The 1954 Third New York Practitioners' Class*, Reel 3, Side 2.

7. Concepts or Is?

1. "Flesh and Flesh," *The 1954 First Portland Practitioners' Class*, Reel 2, Side 1.
2. "The Word and Words," *The 1954 First Portland Practitioners' Class*, Reel 2, Side 2.

8. Attaining Dominion Through *I*

1. "Attaining Grace," *The 1963 Princess Kaiulani Sunday Series*, Reel 1, Side 1.
2. "Attaining Dominion Through *I*," *The 1963 Princess Kaiulani Series*, Reel 1, Side 2.

9. THE MYSTIC AND HEALING

1. "No Power," *The 1958 Second Sydney and Melbourne Closed Class*, Reel 2, Side 2.
2. "Spiritual Healing," *The 1952 First Honolulu Closed Class*, Reel 4, Side 1.
3. "The Christ: Message and Mission," *The 1958 First Chicago Closed Class*, Reel 4, Side 2.

10. DOMINION THROUGH DAILY REALIZATION

1. "Protective Work," *The 1960 Denver Closed Class*, Reel 1, Sides 1 and 2.
2. "A Blueprint for Study," *The 1960 Denver Closed Class*, Reel 2, Side 1.

11. AWAKENING TO THE SOUL-FACULTIES

1. "The Temple or Sanctuary," *The 1961 Los Angeles Closed Class*, Reel 1, Side 1.
2. "Release God and Man," *The 1961 New York Open Class*, Reel 1, Side 2.
3. "Evolving Our Spiritual Capacities," *The 1961 Los Angeles Class*, Reel 2, Side 1.
4. "The Soul of Man," *The 1961 Hawaiian Village Open Class*, Reel 4, Side 2.
5. "The Mystical Approach," *The 1961 Mission Inn Closed Class*, Reel 4, Side 1.

12. CONSCIOUSNESS UNFOLDING AS THE HARMONY OF OUR EXPERIENCE

1. *The 1963/1964 Christmas-New Year's Message*, Reel 1, Side 1.
2. "Mystic Law," *The 1958 First Chicago Closed Class*, Reel 4, Side 1.

INDEX

In each entry, the number before the colon indicates the page number, the number following the colon indicates the paragraph on that page.